Affleck

Potlatch as Pedagogy

Learning Through Ceremony

Potlatch as Pedagogy
Learning Through Ceremony

Sara Florence Davidson and Robert Davidson

PORTAGE & MAIN PRESS

© 2018 by Sara Florence Davidson and Robert Davidson

Excerpts from this publication may be reproduced under licence from Access Copyright, or with the express written permission of Portage & Main Press, or as permitted by law.

All rights are otherwise reserved and no part of this publication may be reproduced, stored in a retrieval system, or transmitted in any form or by any means—electronic, mechanic, photocopying, scanning, recording or otherwise—except as specifically authorized.

Portage & Main Press gratefully acknowledges the financial support of the Province of Manitoba through the Department of Sport, Culture & Heritage and the Manitoba Book Publishing Tax Credit, and the Government of Canada through the Canada Book Fund (CBF) for our publishing activities.

Printed and bound in Canada by Friesens
Design by Relish New Brand Experience

Photo credits: p. 3: Jason Shafto; p. 4 (map) John Broadhead; p. 5: Image B-03590 courtesy of the Royal BC Museum and Archives; cover flap, p. 8: Farah Nosh; pp. 24, 33, 56, 59: Ulli Steltzer; front cover, p. 26: Kenji Nagai ; pp. 39, 48, 50: City of Vancouver Archives/ Dave Paterson; p. 42: Val Embree; p. 51: Mike Poole; p. 53: Anthony Carter

Library and Archives Canada Cataloguing in Publication

Davidson, Sara Florence, 1973-, author
    Potlatch as pedagogy : learning through ceremony / by Sara Florence Davidson & Robert Davidson.

Includes bibliographical references.
Issued in print and electronic formats.
ISBN 978-1-55379-773-9 (softcover).--ISBN 978-1-55379-774-6 (PDF).--ISBN 978-1-55379-775-3 (EPUB)

    1. Haida Indians--Education--British Columbia. 2. Haida Indians--British Columbia--Rites and ceremonies. 3. Potlatch--British Columbia. I. Davidson, Robert, 1946-, author II. Title.

E99.H2D285 2018   971.1004'9728   C2018-904179-X
                                              C2018-904180-3

22 21 20 19   1 2 3 4 5

1-800-667-9673
www.portageandmainpress.com
Winnipeg, Manitoba
Treaty 1 Territory and homeland of the Métis Nation

For the Elders who kept our ancestral knowledge alive through the dark times and the children who will use this knowledge to bring light to the world.

Contents

Foreword	ix
Acknowledgments	xiii
Introduction	1
Chapter 1: Two Working Together	7
Chapter 2: The Story of *sk'ad'a*	11
Learning Emerges from Strong Relationships	14
Learning Emerges from Authentic Experiences	14
Learning Emerges from Curiosity	15
Learning Occurs through Observation	16
Learning Occurs through Contribution	17
Learning Occurs through Recognizing and Encouraging Strengths	18
Learning Honours the Power of the Mind	18
Learning Honours History and Story	20
Learning Honours Aspects of Spirituality and Protocol	20
Differing Pedagogies	21
Chapter 3: "We Were Once Silenced"	23
We Were Once Silenced	26
The Potlatch Ban	27
The Indian Agent	30
Residential Schools	31
Connecting to *sk'ad'a*	34

Chapter 4: "Celebrating one more time in a way they knew how"   35
    Haida Pole Raising   36
    Connecting to sḵ'ad'a   45

Chapter 5: "That Pole Doesn't Belong to You Anymore"   46
    Preparing to Raise the Pole   46
    Connecting to sḵ'ad'a   53

Chapter 6: Born "in the Nick of Time"   55
    Charles Edenshaw Memorial Longhouse Feast (1978)   56
    Tribute to the Living Haida Feast (1980)   58
    Children of the Good People (1981)   58
    Every Year the Salmon Come Back (1989)   62
    Memorial for Arlene Nelson and Arnold Davidson (1992)   63
    Urban Feasts (1993/1994)   63
    Gyaa 'isdlaa (2016)   64
    Redistribution of Knowledge   65
    Connecting to sḵ'ad'a   66

Chapter 7: Potlatch as Pedagogy   67
    Learning Emerges from Strong Relationships   68
    Learning Emerges from Authentic Experiences   68
    Learning Emerges from Curiosity   69
    Learning Occurs through Observation   70
    Learning Occurs through Contribution   71
    Learning Occurs Through Recognizing and Encouraging Strengths   72
    Learning Honours the Power of the Mind   72
    Learning Honours History and Story   72
    Learning Honours Aspects of Spirituality and Protocol   73
    The Paper Bag   74

Appendix A: Feasts and Potlatches Hosted and Co-Hosted by Robert Davidson   77

References   79

Foreword

I write this foreword to *Potlatch as Pedagogy: Learning Through Ceremony* on the unceded and shared lands of the xʷməθkʷəy̓əm (Musqueam), Skwxwú7mesh Úxwumixw (Squamish), and Tsleil-Waututh Indigenous Peoples. The authors, Sara Florence Davidson and Robert Davidson of Haida ancestry, a daughter and father team, have created a compelling book of powerful memories, stories, teachings, and potential educational practices. As an Indigenous educator and scholar, I participated in Sara's academic journey in the role of committee member for her doctoral thesis. She has also worked with me on other research and writing projects. A great passion that we both share relates to appreciating the power and beauty of traditional and life experience stories to educate the heart, mind, body, and spirit. I am also a great admirer of the way that her father, Robert, an internationally renowned artist, tells stories through his art. The authors invite us, as readers, to learn about Haida ways of knowing, to appreciate the struggles to keep this knowledge alive in peoples' hearts and minds despite years of colonization that outlawed such knowledge, and to consider ethical and relevant ways to bring Indigenous knowledge and Indigenous pedagogies into educational and community sites.

The Davidsons share nine Haida sk̲'ad'a, principles that form a foundation of learning and teaching: strong relationships; authentic experiences; curiosity; observation; contribution; recognizing and encouraging strengths; honouring the power of the mind; Indigenous history and stories; as well as spirituality and protocol. These principles emerged from stories remembered and told by Robert about ways that he learned from family and community members, from living Haida culture every day, and from gaining personal and collective insights about learning and teaching. The process of remembering and revitalizing Haida knowledge, values, and practices has been a difficult struggle. But, finally, the time has come when Canadian society, and those involved in education in particular, are encouraged to learn about Indigenous peoples' history and how their Indigenous knowledge can be included in various levels of education.

The 1996 Royal Commission on Aboriginal Peoples and the 2015 Truth and Reconciliation Commission of Canada recommended that all Canadians need to understand the impacts of colonial history, law, and policy that denied generations of Indigenous people core Indigenous practices such as the Potlatch and other cultural ceremonies. The Davidsons' book exceeds these recommendations. They tell stories of this sad part of colonial history – yet, the resistance and resilience of Haida people to keep this knowledge going is a truly inspirational story.

Other true stories are shared about carving and raising a Haida pole in 1969 in the Haida community of Massett, the first in almost 100 years; re-introducing various feasts and potlatches; and re-creating carved masks, songs, and dances. These stories show that through commitment, careful individual and collective remembering, and working cooperatively traditional Haida and Indigenous knowledge can be revitalized and can thrive.

The sk'ad'a principles are presented twice in the book, first as a form of Indigenous knowledge that Robert received from his family, community, and his own learning. Second, Sara presents the same principles as a form of pedagogy to show the threaded connection between the stories/knowledge and ways that educators can consider these concepts to inform and strengthen their teaching practice.

In addition to the learning relationship between Sara and Robert that shows the power of intergenerational teaching and learning (as pedagogy), there are lessons about research ethics and methodology. Their robust learning and research relationship results in working respectfully, responsibility, and reverentially with Haida stories and knowledge, which exemplifies a sturdy ethical research process. The innovative presentation of personal life experience stories has lessons for graduate students and faculty related to documenting, making meaning, and sharing research understandings through these stories. However, this book has another very important implication.

Often, the loss or denial of Indigenous language, knowledge, values, and practices may seem too overwhelming to change. One may question how an individual can make a difference. The story of how Robert, as a young adult made a commitment to bring back Haida forms of art and how his family and community supported and challenged him throughout the years to continue with Haida revitalization of songs, dances, and ceremonies have important leadership, family, and community development lessons.

One of the core strategies that has guided my educational work over the years, and to which I have a firm commitment, is to embed Indigenous knowledge and stories in educational sites in meaningful ways to result in quality education. *Potlatch as Pedagogy: Learning Through Ceremony*, is an excellent exemplar of this approach that braids stories, Indigenous knowledge approaches, and action together for many uses. Educators, academics, post-secondary students, community members, artists, and many others who read this book will be hosted to an unforgettable potlatch of ideas and considerations that will feed your heart, mind, body, and spirit.

Respectfully
Dr. Jo-ann Archibald – Q'um Q'um Xiiem
Stó:lō and St'at'imc First Nations

Acknowledgments

Haw'aa to *Naanii* and *Tsinii* (Florence and Robert Davidson Sr.) for their unending guidance and support. To *Tsinii*, for the many ancient songs and stories, teaching me to carve, and connecting me with ceremony. To *Naanii*, for her teaching about feasting, potlatching, and for fine-tuning our songs. *Haw'aa* to my grandparents' generation, who were hosted by *Naanii* and *Tsinii*, and came together many times to solidify their memories of our history to guide the totem-pole raising. *Haw'aa* to Mom and Dad (Vivian and Claude Davidson) for their great support. To Dad, for his direction with carving and his many stories that continue to guide me. To Mom, for her constant encouragement. *Haw'aa* to Susan Davidson who gave me much needed support. *Haw'aa* to my s*k*aanalang, my father's sisters, Virginia Hunter, Emily Goertzen, Primrose Adams, Myrtle Kerrigan, Agnes Davis, Merle Andersen, and Clara Hugo, who were always there to help *Naanii* and *Tsinii*. *Haw'aa* to my uncles, Uncle Victor Adams and Uncle Alfred Davidson, who gave me unending guidance and advice on ancient knowledge. *Haw'aa* to *skil qaat'la.aas* Reg, my brother, for being a pillar of support for all the events I have hosted and co-hosted, whether it was fishing for food for the potlatches and feasts or being a sounding board and giving guidance. *Haw'aa* to my wife Terri-Lynn for her support and insight on cultural knowledge, law, and ceremony and for keeping me organized. *Haw'aa* to my children, Sara and Ben, my niece Leslie, my nephew Cecil, and their generation for their commitment to learning and practicing our traditions. *Haw'aa* to Sara for the beautiful way she put these stories into words.

—RCD

Haw'aa to my father, Robert, for his endless commitment to this project. He always made time for all of my questions – answering each one in interviews, emails, texts, and phone calls, regardless of the time of day. His tireless work reviewing the transcripts and the manuscript to clarify his ideas and to ensure accuracy made this book possible.

Haw'aa to my mother, Susan, for reading the manuscript and providing me with valuable feedback and for her commitment to supporting me to strengthen my connection to my Haida ancestry throughout my life. *Haw'aa* to my brother, Ben, for encouraging me and for always providing inspiration through his art.

Haw'aa to my stepmother, Terri-Lynn, for reviewing the manuscript and providing research support. *Haw'aa* to Joanne Yovanovich, Tanisha Salomons, and Walker Brown for their additional research contributions.

Haw'aa to Christine Bridge, Maryann Thomas, and Michael Woods for reading early versions of the manuscript and sharing their thoughts with me.

Haw'aa to Jo-ann Archibald – Q'um Q'um Xiiem for the gift of her good words at the beginning of this book. *Haw'aa* to Carl Leggo for his ongoing support to embrace my creativity and for always encouraging me to write. *Haw'aa* to Bryan Brayboy for providing the opportunity to begin writing this story.

Haw'aa to Garry Thomas Morse, for his help to clarify my ideas and finetune my words. *Haw'aa* to Catherine Gerbasi, who first approached me to ask about my work and to Highwater Press for believing in this project and supporting the vision and intention of this work.

Haw'aa to my partner, Angus, who has supported me in every possible way to complete this book, from making me the perfect cup of tea to listening to every single idea regardless of the hour.

And *haw'aa* to all of you who have supported and encouraged me while writing this book. Your words and your belief in this work carried me through whenever I felt uncertain.

—SFD

Introduction

Dii tuulang Kuyaa 'isis[1], my precious friends, my name is Sara Florence Davidson. My father is Robert Davidson. He is of Haida and Tlingit ancestry. His name is *Guud san glaans* which means "eagle on whom it is dawning." My mother is Susan Davidson. She is *'waasdan janaas*[2], and she was given the name *Nan st'laay tuwaa Kwiiwaas*, which means "precious greasy hands," by my great-grandmother, Florence Davidson. My surname, Davidson, comes to me indirectly through the missionaries. They assigned my great-grandfather the name David and used his Haida name *Naahlaang* as his surname. My great-grandfather was the son of David Naahlaang and was thus given the last name Davidson, which was passed to my grandfather, my father, and then onto me. The missionaries did not observe or respect that we are matrilineal and our names are intended to be passed on to us through our mothers. According to Bob Joseph (2018), "Traditional names went against the government's objectives; the government feared that leaving Indigenous people with their traditional names would take away their motivation to assimilate" (35).

The Haida have two moieties or social groups, Raven and Eagle, and each moiety is made up of different Clans. Traditionally, we only married members of the opposite moiety, often the Clan of our father. Because we are matrilineal, our Clan comes from our mother when we are born. My father is an Eagle who belongs to the *Ts'aahl* Clan. My great-grandmother adopted my mother into the *Yahgu janaas* Raven Clan, which gave my brother and me a place in Haida society.

---

1 The orthography for the Haida words used in this book has been agreed upon as the working standardized orthography of all three dialects based on orthography meetings at the three dialect Haida language gatherings. They were graciously provided by JasKwaan A. Bedard

2 The Haida word for "Washington Lady" (a woman of European ancestry)

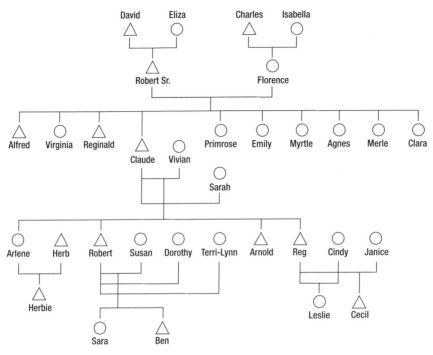

Davidson family tree (partial)[3]

One of the names that my great-grandmother gave me is *SGaann jaadgu san glans*, which means "killer whale woman on whom it is dawning." I use this name in my work because it acknowledges my connection to my father, just as my Clan connects me to my mother. In this way, my work draws on the strengths of the *'waasdan janaas* that come to me through my mother and the strengths of the Haida that come to me through my father.

Though my father was born in Hydaburg, Alaska, he was raised in the community of Old Massett[4], which is on the northern coast of Haida Gwaii, a remote archipelago located off the northwestern coast of British Columbia. According to European history, Haida Gwaii and the Haida were "discovered" by explorers seeking trade opportunities in the late 18th century. In 1852, the Hudson's Bay Company arrived seeking gold, and in 1876, Archdeacon Collison, the first missionary to work on Haida Gwaii, established himself in Massett (Harrison 1925). However, according to our own history, the Haida were discovered by Raven or *Nang Kilslaas* when he was travelling all over the earth. During his

---

3   A more detailed family tree can be found in Blackman (1982).

4   In this book, Old Massett and Massett are used interchangeably to refer to the village located on the reserve, while New Masset and Masset are used interchangeably to refer to the village located 2km south of the reserve.

travels, he found a cockleshell that was being tossed about in the waves. When he approached the shell to see what it was, he discovered that inside the cockleshell there were many children (Edenshaw, as cited in Swanton 1905b).

Raven and the First Men, by Ben Davidson

It is difficult to know the exact population of the Haida before European contact and specifically before 1835 when the Hudson's Bay Company was directed to take censuses of the nations with whom they were in contact. We do know that the population was significantly greater than what was recorded in 1835, because by that time Indigenous peoples in British Columbia had been in contact with Europeans, who introduced foreign diseases, for several decades (Duff 1997). Smallpox was one such disease that came close to eradicating the Haida population – particularly during the outbreak of 1862, which began in Victoria and was predominantly carried back to the nations along the coast and spread throughout those regions (Boyd 1999). According to my great-grandmother, her mother Isabella Edenshaw narrowly escaped that epidemic when it reached Haida Gwaii (Davidson, as cited in Blackman 1982); however, many were not so fortunate. When I asked my father about the impact of smallpox on the Haida, he described a potlatch, hosted by the late *Kwakwaka'wakw*[5] artist and chief Beau

---

5 "Kwak'wala-speaking peoples" whose traditional and unceded territory is located near the north end of what is currently known as Vancouver Island, the surrounding islands, and the adjacent mainland.

Dick, that took place in 2008. The potlatch was to honour the 300 Haida people who died of smallpox in the *Kwakwaka'wakw* territory, as they tried to make their way home from Victoria.

One Haida population estimate indicates that in 1835, there were 6000 Haidas, which dropped to 800 in 1885, with a population low of 588 in 1915 (Duff 1997). Other Haida population estimates were 9490 before 1836, 8428 in the 1830s, 1598 from 1880-1883, and 1049 from 1915-1920 (Boyd 1999).

The impact of this rapid population decline resulted in Haida people relocating from their original village sites to larger combined villages. This amalgamation of villages containing so many different Clans presented new challenges for the Haida social structure. As Marianne Boelscher describes it,

> The village of Masset is … atypical of aboriginal Haida villages, as members of more than a dozen lineages lived here, who in pre-contact times would not have shared a village, and would rarely have engaged in daily interaction or ceremonial obligation (1989, 25).

In 1882, the joint reserve commission "allocated only abandoned and present village sites as reserve land" (Boelscher 1989, 13), and by the 1900s, settlements only existed in Skidegate and Old Massett (Boyd 1999) or *Gad Gaaywaas*.

In 1884, the Potlatch Ban was enacted, which made it illegal for the Haida and other First Nations to host potlatches in the region that is currently known as Canada. Traditionally, the potlatch was the legal foundation of our social structure and ensured the transmission of our cultural knowledge, as "among the Haida, all claims

Haida Gwaii

to social position must be witnessed and sanctioned by the public" (Boelscher 1989, 6). These cultural aspects of the potlatch were grossly misunderstood by the missionaries. For example, as Charles Harrison (1925, 53) described, "The potlatch was another custom of the old Haidas. The potlatch was the impoverishing native custom of giving away property and has now been discontinued." In fact, the potlatch raised the social standing of the host and his family and *increased* their "wealth."

Four Haida men in ceremonial regalia at Massett, 1881.

For nearly five decades, my father has worked to relearn our traditional Haida ceremonies from Haida Elders and used the potlatch as a way to share and redistribute this knowledge following the repeal of the Potlatch Ban in 1951. Though the story is written from my perspective, it is based on stories that my father has shared with me over the years in order to teach me more about our family's and our nation's history. I have acknowledged his commitment to learning and his tremendous contributions to this book by identifying him as an author, because I recognize that without his perspective and his guidance, there would not have been a story to share.

In Chapter 1, I describe the process through which my father and I created this book, and in Chapter 2, I describe the *sk'ad'a* principles that are based on previous work with my father (Davidson & Davidson 2016).[6] In Chapter 3, I describe how we nearly lost our traditional knowledge because of laws that were enacted by the Canadian government in a blatant attempt to assimilate us and eliminate our Haida identities. In Chapters 4 and 5, I describe the story of the first totem pole to be carved and raised in Old Massett in nearly a century. In Chapter 6, I describe some of the potlatches and feasts that my father has hosted and describe how he used those events to share what he had learned about ceremony and protocol. In Chapter 7, I use the sk'ad'a principles as a framework to describe how my father shared his knowledge with the community and used these principles in the feasts and potlatches that he hosted to share his knowledge with the community. I also describe some of the implications for contemporary classroom practice.

I would like to state very clearly that I am sharing this story, with my father's permission, to strengthen our understanding of traditional pedagogies, or sk'ad'a. However, this story belongs to my father and his family and community. This story is being shared to support us, as educators, to continue to move forward in honour of my father's belief that the sharing of knowledge helps us to grow.

This story is not an invitation to replicate my father's actions or undertakings, nor is it an invitation to host a potlatch. Rather, it is an invitation to learn about the knowledge he received from his family and community. It is an invitation to reflect on how some of his approaches to learning and teaching might be applied in the classroom. Furthermore, it is an invitation to consider how we might add more depth and meaning to the ways in which we bring Indigenous perspectives, knowledge, and pedagogies into our classrooms.

---

[6] This chapter is based on an article previously published in the *Canadian Journal of Education*, Davidson & Davidson (2016).

1

Two Working Together

My father is a Haida artist who began carving at the age of 13. For nearly six decades, he has contributed to the revival of Haida art[7]. As an artist, he carefully observes the world and translates what he sees and learns into colours and shapes, such as ovoids, U shapes, and tri-negs. As an educator, I also observe the world carefully, but I translate what I see into words and stories. My father refers to the shapes that he uses as the Haida alphabet, an insight that came to him when he looked at a picture I had drawn as a young child. The picture (right) consists of shapes and letters of the alphabet, and he says that when I drew it, I explained to him that "the alphabet is the doorway to the other side…" As an educator, I have seen the barriers that are created for students who have challenges with print literacy. For these students, mastering "the alphabet" or print

Alphabet drawing by Sara

---

7   See Steltzer, Ulli and Robert Davidson. *Eagle Transforming: The Art of Robert Davidson*. Vancouver, BC: Douglas & McIntyre, 1994.

literacy allows students to pass through "the doorway to the other side." Today, when I look at the drawing, I see it as a representation of the space where my father and I both connect and diverge: we both see the world and feel compelled to share how we understand it, but my father uses shapes to form images whereas I use letters to form words.

My father created the painting on the cover of this book. It is called *hlGed sda sGwaansang,* which means "closely related" or "two working together," like a bow and arrow. The first time I saw this painting in my father's studio and heard what it symbolized, I knew it would be the cover of this book. He explained that the painting represented the bow and arrow, or "two working together," and this is the way in which my father and I work together.

Years ago, I attended an event hosted by another nation. Our traditional Haida dance group, the Rainbow Creek Dancers, had been invited to perform. Unfortunately, many members of our group were unable to attend the event, and only a few of us were present that day. When the time came for us to sing our songs, it dawned on me that I did not truly know the words to the songs. Though I had been singing them since I was a child, in that moment, I suddenly realized that I only knew how to follow our songs and not how to lead them. This moment of awareness led me to wonder what would happen to these songs when our leaders were no longer with us. What would happen when the time came for me to lead these songs?

Sara and Robert Davidson in the studio.

When I returned home, I asked my father if he would teach me some of the songs well enough to lead them. I worked closely with him to learn the words and the meanings and the protocols associated with them. To learn the Haida songs, I would listen carefully to my father singing them, and then I would practice singing them alone. Later, I would return to my father and sing the songs for him. He would listen to me sing and tell me when I was making a mistake, correcting me when necessary. This was the way my father taught me the songs. This was the way I made sure I was learning the songs correctly.

My father believes that we are "all connected to the past by a thin thread. And when we come together as a group, then those threads form quite a thick rope" (Davidson in Steltzer & Davidson 1994, 99). I learned those songs because I did not want to be the one to weaken the rope that connects us to our ancestors.

This story is one of the threads that I hold.

It is my responsibility to ensure that this story accurately reflects my father's perspectives, even after it has been woven together with my own understandings and interpretations. To honour this responsibility, I have based this story upon a series of interviews that I conducted with my father in his studio between 2014 and 2018[8]. I recorded the interviews and then transcribed them to enrich my own understanding of our conversations. I also forwarded the transcripts to my father, so that he could review them as well. During the interview that followed, my father would inform me of any corrections or clarifications he wanted made to the previous transcripts. Once I had finished the series of interviews, I wrote about the meaning I had made from my father's stories, and my father reviewed what I had written to ensure that I was accurately representing the information he had shared with me – that I had captured the *intention* of his stories. This is how he taught me through his stories. This is how I made sure I was representing his stories correctly.

When I asked my father about the painting on the cover of this book, he spoke of the two faces that he saw in the shapes and the thin black lines that he considered to be lines of communication. As two of us were working on this project, our success relied upon our ability to communicate with one another. My father also explained to me that the red and black colours came from before European contact in the late 18th century, and some of the stories my father shared were about the time before contact. The blue and yellow colours are from

---

[8] Excerpts from these interviews have been included throughout this book. Extensive quotes appear in a contrasting text style.

after contact, and many of the stories that he shared with me were about the time after contact.

When I look at the painting, I see a merging of the past and the present. I see my father as the red foundation – a connection to our past and what is behind us, and I see myself as the blue, being held up by his knowledge. This connection between the past and the present is reminiscent of one of my *tsinii*'s[9] teachings: we have to look back once in a while to see where we came from, so that we can always find our way back.

The importance of our connection to our past is emphasized in my father's artistic exploration of the supernatural being, Greatest Echo, who had the ability to echo the past and bring it into the present (Davidson, as cited in Sealaska, 2015). According to my father, we are still relearning our history and echoing the past from our ancestors. Each generation is responsible for learning the knowledge of the previous generation and making it meaningful in the present.

Without my father's generation that was born in the "nick of time," there would be no foundation for our present knowledge and understanding of Haida culture and ceremony. Without the younger generation, the knowledge could not continue to live. Together, we can propel the arrow into the sky and reach much farther than we could if we did not have one another. In this way, my father and I are two working together.

---

[9] Haida word for "grandfather"

2

The Story of sk̲'ad'a

This project began long before I even knew that it had started, when my brother and I were much younger. My father took us to visit a couple we had not previously met. They had taken my father into their home when he traveled from Old Massett to Vancouver in 1965 to complete high school. They understood the importance of fostering relationships to encourage his academic success, and in doing so, they supported him to successfully complete his final year of high school.

My father had to travel to Vancouver to complete high school when the local high school in New Masset stopped offering grades 11 and 12 due to dwindling numbers. The story of his journey has remained with me over the years. When I asked him about it during our conversations, my father said that the decision to continue his education, despite the distance from his home community, had to do with his own father.

> It had to do with Dad's coaching me, encouraging me that I had to finish high school, so that became my goal. When they discontinued grade 11 and 12, I was moving from grade 11 to 12 then, I didn't even question that I would go away to finish high school. I didn't even doubt it.

My father explained to me that he visualized finishing high school, but he never thought about the process or how he might achieve it.

Many years later, I became an educator in the K–12 public education system. My career began on Haida Gwaii working mainly with Haida students, before I moved to Whitehorse, where I worked predominantly with First Nations students from communities throughout the Yukon. In each of these locations, I noticed that many of the Indigenous students were experiencing challenges in the academic setting. I did not blame them for their "inability to succeed" or assume that they needed to conform to Eurocentric educational expectations, because I understood that mainstream educational practices were failing to meet the needs of these Indigenous students. As I struggled, and often failed, to find ways to support these students, I became increasingly interested in what had transpired to motivate my father to complete high school so far away from home. I believed that his story could hold part of the key to better supporting Indigenous students. As my difficulties continued, I decided to return to graduate school to learn more about how to better engage and support my students. There, I took many courses seeking answers to my questions, but I was unable to find the knowledge that I sought.

I finally decided to approach my father in the hope of understanding how his experiences with learning might be able to help me to improve the way in which I worked with students in my classes. In asking my father about his life, I was embracing an older practice, that of seeking guidance from Elders and knowledge keepers instead of from books and courses.

Though my father does not classify himself as an Elder, he recognizes that the people who used to guide him with their knowledge are now gone. My father grew up among the Elders when he was young, and he found comfort in their presence. When he spent time with his grandparents, they always reminded him to help the Elders.

> They said to help the old people, so I was continually being reminded of that. So when I saw an older person, for example there was a blind lady, she had a woodshed, and there was a path going between her woodshed and her house. And when I'd be walking down the path, and I saw her chopping wood, I would ask her if she needed help, and I'd scare her every time. "Ah! *Giistuu dang iijang*?" Who are you? And I'd tell her my name, and she'd get all excited. And I said, "Do you need help?" And she'd say yes, so I would. She had a chopping block and whatever wood she was chopping on top of it, she would just feel it where it is and swing her axe and chop it. And so I would chop it for her, and when I made a big pile, I would pack it into the house. And she already had a pile of wood in the house stacked about two thirds of the ceiling height, so she kept herself busy. And several times I seen her, she wanted to go visit one of her relatives on the other end of the village, and she would use her cane and tap the edge of the sidewalk on the way there. If I saw her I would help her or someone else would help her, guide her where she wanted to go.

My father's comfort in the presence of the Elders led to a familiarity with their ways and their stories. Now, he draws on that knowledge to act as a liaison between the ways of those Elders and the ways of today. My father has never taken this role lightly; he spends a lot of his time remembering what the Elders taught him and reading what has been written about Haida history and protocol in order to further expand his understanding.

My father is generous with his knowledge and shares what he knows whenever he is asked to do so. He believes that sharing our knowledge allows us to gain new insights and that withholding information stunts our ability to grow. My father often shares what he knows with me through the stories that he tells. In the past, I listened to these stories in the hopes of better understanding him as a daughter seeks to know her father; however, when I worked with him on this project, I listened to his stories differently. The more time I spent with my father's stories, the more I could appreciate the truth in Jo-ann Archibald's (2008) observation that "in the oral tradition the listener/learner is challenged to make meaning and gain understanding from the storyteller/teacher's words and stories, which is an empowering process" (56).

I am reluctant to admit it now, but initially, I went to my father seeking a list of teaching strategies to use with Indigenous students to support their academic success. I quickly realized, however, that my father would not provide me with such a list. Instead he offered me stories of his childhood intertwined with traditional Haida stories, and reflections on what had made him the success that he is today. As I listened, I understood that it was up to me to take the time required with those stories to understand what they could teach me (Archibald 2008). As I spent time with his stories, themes began to emerge. These themes helped me to understand how he was taught and also how he learned when he was away from school. These themes evolved to become the sk'ad'a principles.

The Haida word for "teach" is *sk'ad'ada*, and the base of the word "teach" is *sk'ad'a*, which means "learn" (J. Bedard, personal communication, May 3, 2018). The connection between these two words reflects my own understanding of teaching – that it is impossible to teach without learning. There are nine *sk'ad'a* principles that teach us from where learning emerges, how learning occurs, and what learning honours. Learning emerges from strong relationships, authentic experiences, and curiosity. Learning occurs through observation, contribution, and recognizing and encouraging strengths. Learning honours the power of the mind, our history, and our stories, as well as spirituality and protocol.

Learning Emerges from Strong Relationships

In all of the stories that my father told me about learning, he was taught by people with whom he had a relationship. As I reflected on his stories, I realized that he was receiving guidance from his grandfather, his uncles, his father – all people for whom he had great respect. For him, the most meaningful learning emerged from those strong connections. In one story that my father shared with me about oversteering a boat, it was clear that his relationship with his uncle enabled him to ask questions to clarify his understanding.

> I wasn't very experienced at steering the boat, so I didn't understand the principles of keeping the boat in a straight line, so whenever I was steering the boat for Dad, I guess I would always oversteer. So we would be zigzagging and Dad would get frustrated with me. He said, "If you went in a straight line, we'll get there quicker!" But it baffled me. I didn't understand how that could be. And so I asked Uncle Alfred, "Dad said that if we went in a straight line, we'd get there quicker. How could that be?" So Uncle Alfred, he said, "Okay, if you got a string and you put wiggles in it, you're going from point A to point B. The wiggles would not reach the destination, but if you stretch the string out then you'd reach it." I said, "Oh wow!" I really liked the way Uncle Alfred was able to explain things. [Now,] I kind of wonder if Dad did set it up too for Uncle Victor to talk to me or Uncle Alfred to talk to me, especially when I was wavering and doing things that went against their values.

My father later explained that he found getting direction from his uncles easier than getting direction from his own father. He remembered being surprised when his cousin said that the opposite was true for him: it was easier to seek guidance from my father's father. My father speculated that this was because being an uncle is different from being a father.

Learning Emerges from Authentic Experiences

In the stories my father shared with me, he related his various learning experiences; he had learned to carve by "carving the other half" of his father's and grandfather's masks and totem poles, he had learned to fish in a boat with his *tsinii*, and he had learned to dig clams on the beach with his uncle.

> [My uncle] would dig the clams, and I would pick up for him – pick up the clams because they are quite fast. Like if you leave them on the beach for any length

of time even five or ten minutes, they'll disappear because they will dig back into the sand. So he would dig the clams and I would pick it up, and in those days they had a box and each box was about 50 pounds. [I would just watch] him dig then I would imitate him and that's how I learned.

Being taught in this authentic way, my father also learned about what he referred to as the subtleties of each activity. Certain techniques that were used to dig the clams became known to him because he was working alongside his uncle. My father also indicated that when he went halibut fishing with his *tsinii*, he learned how to be attentive to shifts in the environment in order to interpret their meaning.

When I went fishing with *Tsinii*, we'd be anchored out, and it would be a beautiful calm day and all of a sudden there's ground swells coming in, rolling in from the north. And *Tsinii* said, "It's going to blow northwest tomorrow." 'Cause that was the prelude to the northwest coming in. The waves came in first before the wind. So there's all these little subtleties [with] being on the land, you learn that language. And I know a lot of that information could get lost if we're not using it.

Marianne Boelscher (1989) also remarked on the importance of knowledge of the winds for the Haida, stating that because we relied upon favourable conditions for our "subsistence pursuits and travels, [we] were and are keen observers and forecasters of wind and weather patterns" (21).

I grew up without understanding the subtleties of which my father spoke. Instead, I have memories of visiting my great-uncle Sam and being impressed by his ability to predict the weather better than the weather channel. At the time, I had no idea that, in the past, his survival had been dependent on this very knowledge.

Learning Emerges from Curiosity

According to my father, he has always been curious. To illustrate this, he shared an insight he had gained about his curiosity when he was a young boy.

I was always curious. For example one of my cousins, he said, "How come you're always taking things apart?" He [couldn't figure out why] I was always taking things apart. He said, "Why do you always take it apart?" But I had no idea [that was how] I was learning about the process at that age.

My father attributes some of his knowledge of Haida art to his curiosity and the questions that he asked as he studied the old pieces. During one of our conversations, he told me that he would study art pieces that had been described as "good" in order to learn more about what made them good, or what made them stand out.

> I always heard about this guy, Pat McGuire. "Oh, he's a wonderful carver." You know people were just praising him up and down for his carving. I really wanted to know what set him apart, and when I saw his work I was blown away by his quality. And having that curiosity, I wanted to be good too. And so having that desire to be good was a motivation.

My father also spoke about the importance of finding the balance between being curious and asking too many questions. My brother and I are familiar with this struggle, and we always knew that we had asked too many questions when my father's response was a loud, short, "*jaa 'ayaa*[10]." Then we knew the conversation was over.

Learning Occurs through Observation

In the stories my father shared with me, he told me about learning from watching his grandfather, his father, his uncles, his cousins, and older children. He would observe and then copy what they did.

> When we played in the woods, for example, I just remember a couple of people I would play with. There were always several of us. We would go into the woods, and they were older than me so they knew more than I did in terms of, for example, how to make a bow. We would make the bows out of cedar branches and the arrow would be made out of cedar like cedar shakes. And we used elderberry branches. The inside of the elderberry branch was soft so we'd cut, little – maybe two or three inches of the branch – and stick the arrow in that soft part and that became the head of the arrow. And I would be copying the older people what they were doing so I would copy on how to make an arrow and how to make a bow.

I have always thought of my father as intelligent, so it surprised me when he told me that in school, he was labeled a slow learner. He attributed the label to the fact that he never rushed to put up his hand the way that the non-Indigenous students in the class did.

---

[10] This is the Haida phrase for "I don't know," but in this context, it was used to signal that the conversation was over.

> That was the other thing I remember, when the students were asked a question, it was always the white kids who had their hand up. Me, me, choose me, choose me. They were all so eager with the answer. We always stood back, but I never understood why. But it wasn't our way. It wasn't our way. So we were labeled as slow learners even though we knew the answer, we didn't race to be chosen.

I believe that part of the reason he did not race to put up his hand was because of the way that he was brought up – not to boast or flaunt his knowledge. Also, learning through observation takes time, and this sort of time is not always provided in the educational situations that take place at school.

Learning Occurs through Contribution

My father explained that the importance of contributing was foundational in his upbringing.

> We always had to contribute. Always, always, always. Chop wood, pack wood in, and when we got to the oil stove my chore was to fill the oil can that fed the stove. And also Dad would beachcomb, so we went up the inlet and we'd beachcomb the beach looking for logs because he was selling firewood. And those logs were big. I remember having to roll them up the beach and having to chop it. And my job was to pile the wood and when I wasn't doing a good job, he'd push it over and say, "You have to redo it," because the firewood was on display. Other people were selling wood too and people would buy the best pile first. And I remember him telling me, he said Captain Brown told him, he said "You have to give them a full cord when they're buying a cord." He said, "If I owed you a dollar, I'm not gonna give you 99 cents." That's what Dad told me. So that was another part of my learning is that you have to give 100%. When you make a commitment, you have to be fully committed.

When he was 13, my father began earning his own money, and he was told that he had to give some of this money to the family to help out. My *tsinii* explained that this was because my father had to earn his own keep because he would not always be there to look after him. However, my father later clarified that the contribution did not always need to be financial.

> It was always instilled in me to give and contribute. And I feel strongly in that, not just financial, but also creatively. Whatever knowledge I have, I give it away whether it's through potlatching or feasting or in my studio. And I think of that as my communal contribution.

My father said that when his own father went fishing, many of the salmon he caught would be given to the Elders. Now, my Uncle Reg has taken on this role; this was how they were brought up.

Learning Occurs through Recognizing and Encouraging Strengths

Through the stories that my father told, I learned that it was not his choice to become an artist. Rather, he attributes his career to the people around him who recognized his artistic talent as a strength and encouraged him to pursue creative endeavours.

> Sam Simpson was working on a schooner. He was the owner of the cannery in New Masset, and Dad would bring these chunks of wood home, and he said, "I want you to start carving now." Like I remember him badgering me. It wasn't a choice I had to make. He just kept on me until I started carving.

This encouragement also took place without my father's knowledge. During one interview, he described carving with his *tsinii*.

> I didn't really have any tools then, so I used whatever tools *Tsinii* wasn't using, and it happened every time. Whatever tool he was using I always wanted to use that one, so as soon as he put it down I'd grab it and start carving away. And *Naanii*[11] told me years later that she encouraged *Tsinii* just to let me use those tools. So there was that going on behind the scenes. Like I wasn't aware that *Naanii* was telling him what to do too.

Learning Honours the Power of the Mind

Since I was very young, my father has always spoken about the power of the mind. Whenever I have found myself facing something difficult, he reminds me *"Guudangang hl tlaats'gaadii"* or "make your mind strong." I always thought that his belief in the power of our minds came from the self-help books that he read when I was a child. But in the stories that my father told, the power of visualization to achieve goals emerged as a theme – and the examples that he drew upon came from his life and our history. In our conversations, my father shared with me countless examples of how he had used the power of his mind to achieve his goals. He spoke of the baskets that he made playing basketball,

---

[11] Haida word for "grandmother"

hosting a feast or a potlatch, and everything from buying a house to earning a bicycle as a boy by collecting bottles, babysitting, and carving argillite.

> One day I was looking through the catalogue, and I saw the bike I wanted, so I had a visual on it. That's the bike I want, and within three weeks I had enough money saved to buy it. So once I had the visual then I was able to accomplish it.

He also shared with me things his own father had told him, including the story of "how the art started."

> [Dad] said there was this person he saw in the water totem poles and the houses. And a voice told him to memorize the totem poles. That's another visual. And so when [that person] went back to the village, he imitated what he remembered and that was the beginning of the totem poles.

Once again, this illustrated the importance of being able to visualize.

In the stories of Raven Traveling (Swanton 1905b), there are many times when Raven uses his mind to manifest his wishes. For example, in a story about Raven and Supernatural fisherman, Raven brought on the wind with the power of his thoughts.

> As soon as Xāusgana [Supernatural fisherman] had gone a hunting Raven went back to the canoe. He lay down in it and thought: "I wish that a wind would start from the island and that the canoe would drift away!" He pulled his blanket over his head and pretended to sleep. Now a wind arose, and the canoe drifted away. (144)

Referring to these ancient stories, my father reminded me that when Raven wanted to get from Point A to Point B, he would get there in one stroke of the paddle. After my father reviewed this section of the book, he also recalled the story about Raven and the crooked tree that was recorded by Swanton (1905a).

> [Raven] came to a crooked tree bending over the beach, and when he was passing it, and saw it, said, "What is the matter with you? What makes your mind crooked? Your mind cannot be like mine, for I have lost my wife." So even until now, they say that people have "crooked minds"… (233)

As my father recalled this story, what resonated for him was the connection between the tree's mind and its crooked shape – once again emphasizing the powerful connection between our mind and our being.

Learning Honours History and Story

For many *Yaats' Xaadee*[12], stories are a source of entertainment, but for us they are also teachers. Throughout my life, my father has used his stories to teach me or to give me advice. There have been many times when my father has looked to the past to help me in the present, and occasionally, he has guided me using advice that comes from our stories of Raven. My father also learned through stories told to him by his own family. During a discussion about "making your mind strong," my father explained to me that the Haida believe our mind resides in our chest.

> Uncle Alfred, in one of his stories to me, he said that when he was a child, Charlie Edenshaw, his *tsinii*, would hold [him] on his lap, and he would cough up phlegm from way down in his chest. And he would rub it on Uncle Alfred's chest as a child. And [Uncle Alfred] didn't understand why, but he had two theories: one [was] to make him a great speaker, which he was, or to make his mind strong. Because [Uncle Alfred] said the Haida believed that's where our mind was because we feel everything there.

I had not heard this before, but it made sense, as it emphasized the proverbial connection between the mind and the heart. It is also interesting to note that the Haida word for *mind* is the same as the Haida word for *throat* (Swanton 1905a). Though we did not discuss it explicitly, I believe that this connection between the heart and mind is integral to much of the education that my father received outside of school.

Learning Honours Aspects of Spirituality and Protocol

In my father's stories about *sḵ'ad'a*, our spiritual beliefs did not exist separately from the transmission of knowledge. Instead they were embedded throughout the stories, forming a vital component of his traditional education. He described hanging fish on the drying racks at the Yakoun River where he went with his family to fish for food. He said that he had been scattering fish all over the drying racks and his father had told him, "You gotta always face the salmon upstream so the spirit will always come back." He also learned to express his gratitude for the salmon.

> When I was leaving the river, the Yakoun River, after canning all the salmon and smoking it, drying it, on the ride up from the camp, up the river to the landing,

---

[12] Haida word for "Iron People" or people of European ancestry.

> I would mentally thank the trees, thank the river, thank the salmon on many of the occasions.

My father also spoke about how his grandfather talked to the halibut that he had caught. Before he clubbed the halibut, he would speak to it like a human.

> He would talk to the halibut [*D'aal ts'ad K̲aagaay*]. Bite the bait. Don't just look at it. I asked Uncle Alfred. I said, "What was *Tsinii* saying to the halibut?" And he said "Bite the bait. Don't just look at it." And when he caught the halibut, he would be talking to it again, and he said "Make your mind strong because I'm going to club you." And so he'd pull the halibut on board and he would rebait the hook and he'd rub the new bait on the eyes of the halibut and he said, "Remember this. Don't just look at the bait. Bite it." And then he'd throw the hook out again and jig some more. So what that was teaching me was the animal kingdom are humans. They didn't treat it lightly. They treated it like humans. (R. Davidson, interview, July 9, 2014 as cited in Davidson & Davidson, 2016, 8)

My father elaborated that his grandfather and their generation did not treat the halibut or other food merely as a product the way we do today.

Differing Pedagogies

The world in which my father grew up is different from the world that I know today. He explained to me that during his grandfather's time, the culture was lived and the knowledge was common. He emphasized that if the knowledge is not used, it gets lost.

> They lived the culture, and it was common knowledge in [my *tsinii*'s] time period. Like they knew the land, they knew the water, they knew the weather. I remember when Dad was looking for a tree, *Tsinii* said, "There's a tree at this..." [and] he would name the spot at Naden Harbour and describe the location. So they had a visual map of where the different trees were because their life relied on it. Being a canoe maker, [*Tsinii*] would know where the trees are. He would have a mental map. And the more I went to the Yakoun River, the more I got to know the river. If I go back there now, I would have to relearn it because it's been so long since I was there. Like when I went fishing with *Tsinii*, he knew when to leave with the tide because you never went against the tide, you always went with the tide. So several times, I went out to Dixon Entrance on the dinghy. He had two sets of oars on there, and I would row on the bow

pulling, and he'd be in the stern pushing his set of oars. And he, you know, as blind as he was, he still looked for the landmarks 'cause what they would do is they would triangulate. Like this point, this point, and they would line points up. Okay, this is where we're gonna fish. So he'd set the anchor and we'd jig for halibut. Sure enough there's fish there. And they had names for those, where the fishing spots were, so they would tell stories to each other.

The stories that my father told me, did not end with the stories that led to the development of the *sk'ad'a* principles. As our conversations continued, he began to tell me about what he learned about Haida ceremony and protocol from the Elders when he decided to raise a totem pole in Old Massett in the late 1960s. However, to understand the significance of what was gained with the pole raising, it is first important to understand what was lost when we were once silenced.

3

"We Were Once Silenced"

My *tsinii* was the chief of our Clan. When I was a child, he used to sing a power song at potlatches. I remember how sad and mournful his voice was as he sang and looked out into the audience. The song was about the treasures a man had lost, and as my *tsinii* sang the song, he looked out into the audience seeking the treasures. According to the Haida Gwaii Singers Society[13] (2008), the song

> was composed when a man was leaving his village and feared that he would lose all of [his] treasures while he was away. He buried all of his treasures in the forest behind the village, only to find them gone when he returned. From this [Power] Song we learn that when we keep our treasures hidden from the rest of the world, we risk losing them (29).

When I sing the song today, I do not look out at the audience. Now, I can close my eyes because we are no longer looking for our treasures in the same way that we had to during my *tsinii's* time.

I was born long after the Potlatch Ban had been lifted. My childhood consisted of journeys between the Lower Mainland and Haida Gwaii – between the homes of my mother, an anthropologist-turned-organic-farmer, and my father, a Haida artist seeking to strengthen cultural connections with our history. For a long time, I was ashamed of my Haida ancestry and did my best to keep it hidden. I associated this part of myself with the negative stereotypes and derogatory labels that were reinforced at school, on television, and in my daily life. While doing research for this book, I learned that my father also had this experience: "When I was a child, I was ashamed to be Haida, like many of my friends. This came from our parents' lack of self-esteem and self-worth, their language and beliefs having been beaten out of them in the residential schools. These same

---

13 My father is a member of the Haida Gwaii Singers Society

feelings were handed down to us (Davidson, as cited in Steltzer & Davidson 1994, 14)."

My father and my uncle have always been committed to the revitalization of Haida culture and ceremonial practices. This commitment was especially apparent when they founded the Rainbow Creek Dancers, a traditional Haida dance group. I was a member of the dance group from a very young age. As a result, I do not remember a time in my life when my Haida culture was not a part of it. I took this for granted, never realizing that there was a time when our ceremonial practices and cultural beliefs were forbidden.

Rainbow Creek Dancers

Historically, the potlatch[14] was used to redistribute wealth in order to establish and maintain social status for Haida people (Blackman 1982; Boelscher 1989; Swanton 1905a) and the potlatch was considered the "final avenue to establishing and upholding social status for the Haida as for other societies of the Pacific Northwest" (Boelscher 1989, 66). Though the Haida had different types of potlatches that served different purposes (Murdock 1936; Swanton 1905a),

---
14 For more detailed information about the Haida potlatch, please see Boelscher, Marianne. *The Curtain Within: Haida Social and Mythical Discourse.* Vancouver, BC: UBC Press, 1989.

according to Boelscher (1989), the struggle to obtain and maintain social power took place at the potlatch.

Potlatch is not a Haida word. Rather, it emerged from a similar word meaning "to give," which became part of the Chinook jargon that was used for trade. A potlatch referred to "any ceremonial distribution of property among different coast peoples regardless of the specific nature of the event" (Steltzer 1984, xii). Our Haida word is *gyaa 'isdlaa*, which means "giving things away" (Boelscher 1989), but we now refer to these events as feasts, potlatches, or doings. As my father explained,

> In the past, people lived by a strict code of laws that was defined by public opinion. Since there were no written documents, all changes to the existing order were made at feasts and potlatches, at a time when the public was present. If you accepted a chieftainship, or you raised a memorial pole, or you got married, all activities were recorded in this way. So when you decided to change the pattern, you had to accumulate the goods to create the potlatch and invite the people. You paid the people of the opposite side for witnessing the change you made. If a person did not come, or did not accept your gift, that was his way of saying, I don't accept what you are doing. You wanted to invite everybody so they couldn't turn around afterwards to squabble about it. (Davidson, as cited in Steltzer 1984, 1)

Margaret Blackman (1977) elaborated that

> The Haida potlatch was, on the one hand, a kind of *rite de passage* in which ritual, formalized distributions of property publicly marked the change in an individual's status: from non-house owner to house chief; from orphan to member of a lineage; from girl to woman; from no status to [*yah Ged*]; from living to dead. (41)

The potlatch was a foundational part of our lives, and our participation ensured the continued transmission of the protocols and ceremonies associated with being Haida. However, the missionaries viewed the potlatch as a significant barrier to their forceful attempts to "civilize" us (*ibid*). According to Marianne Boelscher (1989), the demise of the Haida potlatch "can be attributed to the federal government's anti-potlatching legislation, the missionaries' influence, and the devastating population decline of the late nineteenth century [predominantly due to smallpox]" (66). The missionaries' erasure of Haida culture and ancestral connections was deliberate and, in some circumstances, complete (Blackman 1977). As a result, there are songs and dances, such as the spirit possession dances, that I will never know because of their desire to "civilize" us.

One of the missionaries' first steps was to stop the dancing and spirit performances that were connected with the potlatch. They worked to achieve this by replacing these ceremonial practices with the singing of hymns (*ibid*). In 1879, William Collison, a missionary in Masset, reported "Dancing has been abandoned and in passing along the village after dark my ear is now often greeted with the Christian hymn or the song of praise" (as cited in Blackman 1977, 47). Furthermore,

> by the 1890s the missionaries had gained considerable ground in their battle against the Haida potlatch. They succeeded in halting the spirit performances; they preached against tatooing [sic] and saw that those who failed to heed their preaching were fined or jailed. (*ibid* 50)

Missionary Charles Harrison (1925) also noted in his book, *Ancient Warriors of the North*, that the Haida potlatch had been discontinued. When the act of hosting and attending potlatches was outlawed, we began to lose this connection to our ancestral knowledge and our identities as Haida became threatened.

We Were Once Silenced

In 2000, my father carved a totem pole which he named, "We Were Once Silenced." I remember the first time I saw it in his studio; it was unlike any pole I had ever seen before. I could not look away. I felt compelled to witness the anguish on the faces of the humans who emerged from the cedar. There are faces on the top and bottom that share a single mouth and tongue. The tongue covers the mouth of the humans who are being swallowed by the single mouth. The agony on the human faces is unmistakable, and their pain can be understood regardless of the viewers' ancestry or understanding of Haida art.

We Were Once Silenced
by Robert Davidson

When I asked my father about the pole, he explained that the faces behind the tongue are male and female who share the same mouth. He went on to describe that the tongue is a colonial vehicle that muted us through laws that were designed to eliminate us. These attempts to eliminate us took many forms; the Potlatch Ban, Indian agents, and residential schools were only a few of the ways that were used.

The Potlatch Ban

In 1884, as an amendment to the Indian Act, the Potlatch Ban was introduced in Canada as an attempt to sever authentic connections to our history, as well as the genuine expressions of our Indigenous identities. "The federal government believed that true assimilation could be attained only by legally abolishing all cultural practices" (Joseph 2018, 48), and they believed that its abolishment would ease conversion of Indigenous peoples to Christianity (*ibid*).

> The government of Sir John A. Macdonald (who called the potlatch "a debauchery of the worst kind") banned the potlatch…on the grounds that it and similar ceremonies encouraged barbarity, idleness and waste, interfered with more productive activities and generally discouraged acculturation. (Francis 1992, 99)

Though the Potlatch Ban was intended to abolish all of our connections to our ancestral knowledge and erase our Haida identity, some of my ancestral knowledge was passed on to me specifically because my ancestors defied the Potlatch Ban and continued to share their knowledge in secret. According to anthropologist Margaret Blackman (1977),

> like their [*Kwakwaka'wakw*] neighbors to the south, the Haida practiced the potlatch in secret. They gave potlatches at abandoned villages and camp sites, and they made every effort to keep potlatches held within the village of Masset a secret. Harrison's public chastisement of the Masset potlatchers in 1884 followed his discovery of a mortuary potlatch which they had tried to hide from him. (48)

Until I began working on this project, it did not really occur to me that my father was alive during the time of the Potlatch Ban. However, when I asked him about it, he replied that in those days he knew nothing about the Potlatch Ban. According to him, no one spoke about it, but he did not understand Haida so if it was spoken about in Haida he would not have known. Still, I believe it was a direct result of the Potlatch Ban that my father did not hear his first Haida song until he was 16 – after the Potlatch Ban had been lifted.

> The first time I heard a Haida song was when I was 16. I had no experience before then with Haida songs or even how they sounded. *Tsinii* was outside doing something and *Naanii* was canning or doing something, and this guy from National Film Board asked if they could sing a song for the film that they were doing on myself carving argillite. And [*Naanii* and *Tsinii*] came into the house and *Naanii* Amanda came in and joined them, or they invited her, and they sang five songs, I think, on tape. And I was so taken by that. That was the first time I ever heard Haida songs. Before then, I never heard it; it was not sung. If it was, it wasn't in my presence.

Later, as my father reflected back on that time, he realized that during the Potlatch Ban we had kept many of our traditions alive through Christmas dinners and picnics. He said that Christmas time was a time of feasts; it was our way of hiding a traditional celebration, and he had seen his *naanii* and *tsinii* do it many times.

> It wasn't until years later that I realized why Christmas was such a big deal. It was their way of hiding a celebration, a traditional celebration. It was under the guise of a Christmas feast, a Christmas dinner. Like for example, *Naanii* and *Tsinii*, they would have 40-80 people in their house. And they'd all be talking Haida, talking about our history, resaying their history. They would literally move all the furniture [out of their living room] and put in tables, chairs, and they would host people. There would be two or three [dinners] in a day, so different families would host the village and they would have long tables in their living room. And that was in place of the potlatch. But I didn't know it until years later why the dinners were so big.

Marianne Boelscher (1989) also drew this conclusion, explaining that during Church Army meetings and Christian holiday feasts

> [the Haida] reinforce and uphold notions of respect and prestige which are central to all [*gyaa 'isdlaa*]. Moreover, they provide an arena for traditional-type speeches in the Haida language, in which verbal claims to status and legitimacy are laid for oneself and granted to others. (66–67)

The Elders spoke Haida at these dinners, and my father was unable to follow the stories as closely as he would have liked. Even so, his feeling was that they were talking about the generation before them, about how they did things. He believes this because the Elders would mention names from that generation. During these dinners, the Elders would talk about their history.

> I'm aware that they talked about their history. They would talk about the last generation. Roger Weir, they would talk about him. They'd mention the English names. And, it was their way of confirming with each other their history. They would verify it through the speeches. "Roger Weir did this...and did that..." And so they would rely on that story to govern their own life.

Another way that our ceremonial practices were preserved was by keeping them hidden. As Margaret Blackman (1977) described,

> My main informant recalled that during her seclusion at first menstruation her mother did not call together her father's sisters for a potlatch but rather distributed the potlatch gifts of washbowls by going from house to house. This tactic of geographically distributing potlatch property rather than publicly disbursing it was one adopted also by the [*Kwakwaka'wakw*]. (48)

By masking the ceremonial practices as other events or hiding them altogether, the Elders managed to preserve some of the old ways long enough to pass them on to my father's generation.

Saving face. During one of our conversations, my father told me a story that had been told to him by his grandmother about a face-saving picnic that took place in the late nineteenth century.

> In the earlier times, her earlier times, *Naanii* talked about a face-saving picnic. In those days it was called a picnic. And she said she was 12 years old then. She was born in 1895 so that dates that picnic in 1907. She said the totem pole at Dadens blew down and someone from my [Eagle] Clan made fun of it. It had a grizzly bear on the bottom, and she poked it in the bum and said, "Let's see if this bear will take a shit" in Haida – like she was poking fun of the totem pole falling down. And Henry Edenshaw, he was the last chief of your [Raven] Clan of that time period, and he heard about it. He had a picnic. *Naanii* called it a picnic, but it was really a face-saving potlatch. And he invited the people down there, and 10 people from my Clan were given money and this was to clear their shame of their totem pole falling.

In contrast to a more Canadian approach, whereby we would be expected to apologize for our transgression and rude behaviour, in this case the chief of the Clan was expected to clear his shame about the pole being ridiculed by making payments to the opposite Clan. In another example of saving face, Margaret

Blackman (1977) described that, "In one instance a high-ranking man was going for firewood in his canoe [sic] tipped over and was rescued by a member of the opposite moiety. The former responded by giving a feast and paying his rescuer" (49).

In his article on Haida potlatches, George Murdock (1936) described the face-saving potlatch:

> Whenever a person of high social status suffers in public a mishap which makes him appear ridiculous or causes him to be laughed at, e.g., tripping and falling at a feast or potlatch where members of other Clans are present, he can 'save face' and prevent all future reference to the mishap by giving a small potlatch. (15)

Saving face was and continues to be very important to the Haida. My father said that the belief in this custom was so strong for my great-grandmother, a Raven, that when she fell onto the floor in her home, she refused to let my uncle, an Eagle, help her up. Instead, she insisted that my uncle phone my great-aunt, another Raven, to come to the house to help her up.

The Indian Agent

> The Potlatch Ban and the Indian Act were mainly reinforced by Indian agents. The Indian agent lived in New Masset, so he had close contact with [the people from Old Massett] and he had an iron fist on people in Massett.

The Indian agent had a strong hold on the Haida, and as my father explained, the laws were strict and intimidating. For example, non-Haida people had to sign in and out when visiting and leaving the reserve. This does not mean the Haida were entirely complacent; my father also told stories that he had heard about people putting curtains over the windows when they wanted to sing Haida songs.

Button blankets. My great-grandmother also spoke of dancing during the time of the Potlatch Ban. When she was a little girl, "people did Indian dances, most of them used shawls, wool shawls, when they danced, not button blankets. Now everyone uses button blankets again" (Davidson, as cited in Blackman 1982, 124). According to my great-grandmother, the

> Haida began making button blankets after the missionaries came, after they quit raising poles. The missionary stopped them from doing it and my grandfather was very sad about it. His son, [Guu.u], suggested to my grandfather

that instead of worrying about totem poles they should make designs on blankets they got from traders and put the traders' buttons around the design. My grandfather agreed with his son, and that's when they made one. I don't know if that was the first one, but that was when they started making button blankets around here. Maybe other people, mainland people, made button blankets before that time. (Davidson, as cited in Blackman 1982, 124)

Residential Schools

The Potlatch Ban was not the only means of attempting to assimilate us. The Canadian government believed that assimilation would be achieved most effectively through residential schools; this was "another Imperial initiative inherited and built upon by the federal government. The first two [residential schools] were opened in the late 1840s in Upper Canada and then a system, national in scope, was adopted in 1879 by Macdonald's cabinet" (Milloy 2008, 5). The last residential school in British Columbia was closed in 1985; however, residential schools continued to operate in Canada with federal funding for another year and the last Indian Residential School in Canada did not close until 1996. The Haida were generally taken to four residential schools: Alberni Indian Residential School, which opened in 1920 and closed in 1973; St. Michael's Indian Residential School in Alert Bay, which opened in 1929 and closed in 1975; Coqualeetza Industrial Institute, which opened in 1861 and closed in 1940; and Edmonton Indian Residential School, which opened in 1924 and closed in 1966.

My *tsinii* was sent to residential school when he was 11 years old. In an unpublished autobiography, he wrote that he could remember the day that he was sent to Coqualeetza Industrial Institute. However, the only detail he included about that day was the fact that he could not speak his language there (Davidson, n.d.). According to my father, like many other survivors, my *tsinii* never spoke about being at the school; he simply stated that he had gone. As a result, I do not know many of the details beyond some of the devastating stories that were shared with me when I was old enough to understand them. I do not know the boy that my *tsinii* was before he was taken away, but I knew the man that he became after he returned. He existed between the worlds of the Haida chief, knowledgeable in protocols and traditional practices, and the worlds of despair, where he often became lost and unreachable to me.

The destruction caused by the residential schools was intergenerational, and my father spoke of the disastrous impact it had on the families of the survivors. Today, we speak more about these intergenerational impacts, as we come to better understand them. But at the time, my father was left to make sense of his father's behavior on his own. During one of our conversations, he spoke about the link between parents and children that was broken when the children were taken away from their families and their homes.

> That link was broken with my parents' generation being taken out of the family circle as children. When they went to residential school, they were removed from learning what their role was in the family unit. And so when they came back to the village, they came back as strangers. It took me a long time, it took me until after Dad died, to start to realize the pain he must've went through being taken away from his family and being in a foreign land and speaking a foreign language. He never spoke about his experience at residential school.

My father does not speak Haida, and I believe this is a direct result of residential schools. According to the Truth and Reconciliation Commission of Canada (2015),

> Residential schools were a systematic, government-sponsored attempt to destroy Aboriginal cultures and languages and to assimilate Aboriginal peoples so that they no longer existed as distinct peoples. English – and to a lesser degree, French – were the only languages of instruction allowed in most residential schools. Students were punished – often severely – for speaking their own languages. (107)

Although my great-grandmother explained to my father that the reason they spoke English to him was because they "didn't want [him] to go through the same things [his] mom and dad went through," my father's inability to speak Haida is a source of tremendous sadness for him. Throughout his life, it has been an ongoing obstacle that has hindered his ability to access his history and develop meaningful connections with his family.

The devastating consequences of losing our Indigenous languages, including negative impacts on self-esteem and self-confidence, and loss of connections with Elders, families, and communities, have been well-documented by First Nations educators and authors (Battiste 2013). According to the Truth and Reconciliation Commission of Canada (2015), "By belittling Aboriginal cultures, the schools drove a wedge between children and parents" (107). In the case of my father and many others, this wedge was also driven between the survivors of residential schools and their own children and grandchildren.

> The damage affected future generations, as former students found themselves unable or unwilling to teach their own children Aboriginal languages and

cultural ways. As a result, many of the almost ninety surviving Aboriginal languages in Canada are under serious threat of disappearing. (*ibid*)

For my father and others, it was particularly painful to be unable to speak Haida, because they were put down for not knowing their language. Though this seems particularly harsh to me, I must remember that the criticism likely emerged from a sense of shame and feelings of inadequacy that the children did not speak the Haida language. The threads connecting those children to our ancestors were broken by the laws that were designed to assimilate us and obliterate our Haida identity.

Reg Davidson performing the Eagle Spirit Dance.

But I cannot get lost in despair. I must also remember the resiliency that my *tsinii* and others demonstrated in their commitment to cultural survival. I must remember that my *tsinii* resisted these attempts to assimilate him by continuing to remain dedicated to sharing our songs and our dances so they would not be lost. So instead, I choose to focus on our resiliency as we continue to work to resist and overcome these attempts to colonize us.

> ### Connecting to sk'ad'a
>
> The Haida Elders honoured the educational role of history and story through their commitment to remembering the old knowledge. They shared stories from previous generations at the picnics and dinners. They also honoured spirituality and protocol by having potlatches in the abandoned village sites; this enabled us to continue with this knowledge today.

4
"Celebrating One More Time in a Way They Knew How"

As a result of the Potlatch Ban, my father grew up in a community that was devoid of Haida art, although he had no idea that it was missing from his childhood. In fact, he did not discover the quality of ancient Haida art until he moved to Vancouver in 1965 to complete high school.

> When I came to Vancouver I was really blown away by the quality of the art. Our art. Because I wasn't exposed to it at home at all. There was no evidence of that when I was a child. In looking at the old pieces, the old totem poles, I was taken aback again because there was absolutely no evidence of those old totem poles in the village – any of the villages that I visited with my parents, namely *Yan*, and *K'aayung*, and in Massett. And I guess the only other quality totem pole was in Skidegate, the Beaver totem pole. And so it always tweaked my curiosity, I was always wanting to understand more. All I saw were fuzzy photographs of the argillite totem poles, and I didn't even know anything about the ovoid, the U shape, and when I saw that [old Haida art in Vancouver], I was awestruck.

My father was so taken with the art he saw in Vancouver that when he returned home he searched for any remaining trace of the art.

> [In Vancouver], I saw all these beautiful totem poles done by the Haida, and when I'd go home there was absolutely nothing. Nothing. In fact on one of the trips back home, I knocked on absolutely every door in the village to see if they had anything, any art left. I found one box.

This empty space that was left in the community, as a result of the removal and destruction of the art, was a motivating factor in my father's decision to carve a pole. From his perspective, the role of the artist is to "fill the void." My father described "the void" as the gaps in our knowledge or our practices. As he explained this to me, I understood that he was referring to the spaces that were left because of various attempts to colonize us. Though the void was not apparent to my father when he left his home community to go to school, it became obvious to him after he began to understand more about who we were before contact.

Haida Pole Raising

While working with the Haida, Margaret Blackman (1977) learned that

> The last totem pole raising at Masset occurred in the early 1890s and informants relate variant accounts of it. Some recalled that, in terms of both wealth distributed and the feasting of guests, this potlatch was a poor one, while another informant stated that a large amount was given out. Despite discrepancies in the oral tradition, photographs of the totem pole erected at the potlatch attest to the poor quality of its carving. In addition, this potlatch ended on a sour note when the father of the children who received tatoos [sic] at the potlatch was arrested by the former missionary, now magistrate, and fined for permitting his children to be tatooed [sic](49).

From the early 1890s until 1969, there were no pole raisings in Old Massett.

The Potlatch Ban was repealed in 1951 which meant that Haida people were allowed to sing and dance in public once again; however, my father noticed that something was still missing from the lives of the Elders. This led to his decision to carve and raise a totem pole in Old Massett in the hope of giving them an opportunity to "celebrate one more time in a way they knew how."

> I used to visit some of the old people. This one time when I went home, I went to visit Auntie Grace and Augustus, we called her Auntie Grace, I don't know why not Uncle. Anyway, I went to see them, and there was a whole bunch of old people sitting in the living room, and I just felt the sadness. And that moment inspired me to carve the totem pole because in my mind I wanted these people, my Elders, to celebrate one more time in a way they knew how, and it was just an intuitive feeling. I had no idea about our history, about being muted, being separated from our song and dance ceremony. There was no indication that I was deprived of that, but the intuitive feeling was to create an occasion for them to celebrate one more time in a way they knew how. That's how I thought of it. And once I made a commitment, I had no idea about the log, I had no idea about how I was going to fund it. I never even carved a totem pole before.

Reflecting on this decision, my father admitted that back then, he had no understanding about the commitment he had made. He laughed at himself, recalling his naivety: "I remember thinking before I carved the totem pole that I was going to teach these people a few things. Little did I know that I wasn't even touching the surface in their knowledge."

My father used to visit his uncle Alfred when he returned home. During one of those visits, he said that if Masset got the log, he would carve a totem pole for the village. About a month before my father began to carve the pole, his father called him up and said, "I found a tree for you." Unfortunately, the tree did not pass my great-grandfather's inspection, as the base was too narrow for the height of the pole. According to my father, *"Tsinii* looked at it and told him it was too small, so he got another one. [Dad] said he spent two weeks in the forest looking for a tree."

Once my father had committed to carving the pole, he said that everything fell into place.

> I made a commitment, visual, mental commitment, and once I made that commitment, the doors kept opening towards making it happen. The year before, in 1968, I was teaching carving in Hazelton, and I had no experience in carving wood. Up to that point I only had experience in argillite. And so when I finally made the commitment, I went to UBC to visit Bill Reid's Haida village, and I would study the carvings there. I'd make a mental visual, I mentally and visually memorized the shapes. And then I went to visit Bill Holm. He had a ten-foot pole in his living room, and I asked him how long it took him to carve that. It was a Haida pole. And he said 120 hours, so I based my carving the totem pole on that measure. And then, unbeknownst to me, Audrey Hawthorn, who was the curator of the Museum of Anthropology, applied for the $3000 grant from the BC Cultural Fund to help me. And at the same time, another artist I consulted with was Doug Cranmer. [I asked him], "What advice do you have for me?" He was an accomplished artist from Alert Bay, and he said, "Don't lose the centre line."

In the spring of 1969, when my father was 22, my parents drove up to Haida Gwaii from Vancouver so that my father could carve the pole. When they arrived in Old Massett, they went to visit my grandparents.

> We went to Mom and Dad's house because the log was in front of their house. We went there for lunch, and I had to walk by the log. I didn't even want to look at it. I was terrified. And after lunch, I looked at the log. I said, "Holy shit, what did I get myself into?" And, I didn't even know how to run a power saw. And I bought one of the cheapest power saws you can get because we didn't even have any money. And anyway, that saw got me through that project.

My father said that the tree was huge and the only thing he knew was that he had to cut the tree in half lengthwise.

> It was a huge tree, and I had no experience at all on what to do first. All I knew is, I had to cut it in half, which I did. Uncle Sam helped me with his power saw. And he helped me to square up the back and then Bobby Collison came and helped me for a couple of days with the sledge hammer to help do the hollowing. And I started in May, so that was sockeye time. And I would go and help *Naanii* and *Tsinii* at the Yakoun on weekends and, you know, *Tsinii* was 89 years old and still fishing. And he said, "When I'm done here, I'm gonna help you," and I just couldn't comprehend that 'cause he was so old and had a hard time walking around. And *Tsinii*, every time would say that. And I knew later on, it was to encourage me to carry on. And a couple times, he said, "You're doing a great thing," but I didn't know what he meant. I had no idea [about] the impact the art had on our culture. But they did. They knew. And finally at the end of *Naanii* and *Tsinii*'s fishing at the Yakoun, I could still see *Tsinii* walking up. He was carrying a hammer and a chisel, and walking up from their house to where Reg and I were carving the totem pole. And, I am embarrassed to this day. I had no idea [about] *Tsinii*'s accomplishments. Like he carved two major dugout canoes and built umpteen fishing boats, one sixty-foot seine boat. And a master carpenter, built their house, and here I was, I was afraid of him ruining my log. And finally about half an hour into [carving], he said, "I can't see." But he still cared.

My father said that even though my Uncle Reg had never carved before, he was willing to learn, and my father appreciated this. My uncle's willingness to help was particularly important because the pole had to be finished by the middle of August, so my mother could to return to school in the fall. To meet this deadline, my father and my uncle worked six days a week for 10-12 hours a day. On Sundays, my father would go and help his *naanii* and *tsinii* to fish at the Yakoun River.

Robert and Reg hold a K̲'awhlaa mask

Today, when my father carves totem poles, he begins by drawing concepts and ideas in his sketchbook. Then he uses those drawings to create maquettes, which are smaller three dimensional models of the poles. These maquettes allow him to calculate the proportions of the design before carving the full-sized poles which can be up to 50 feet tall. When he created the pole in 1969, he did it from a drawing that was roughly based on a fuzzy photograph of an old pole from Massett.

This first pole was intended to be a gift to the whole village, and he wanted to make it "neutral;" however he later reflected that this was very naïve.

> At that time, I didn't have very much cultural knowledge, but I wanted this to be a neutral totem pole for the whole village. Now, I know that it's a Raven Clan pole, since the Grizzly Bear, the main character of this pole, is a crest of the Raven Clan. The only way it could have been neutral was to have crests from both Eagle and Raven Clans on there (Davidson, as cited in Steltzer & Davidson 1994, 22).

In the beginning, there was not a lot of community support for the pole. My father attributed this to the many broken promises that had previously been made in the village.

> There was a lot of doubt in the beginning. You know, there's so many promises all the time. And here's this young kid promising to carve a pole, and so there wasn't much support other than from Mom and Dad, *Naanii* and *Tsinii*, Uncle Victor was carving a canoe then, but it was more them and Susan.

Some people also wanted to know why my father wanted to bring up the past.

> Some Haida people asked me, "Why do you want to bring up the past?" We were the children of survivors. We had lost 95 percent of our population; in the 1910 census, there were 600 Haida, compared to some 10,000 to 17,000 at contact. The laws did not permit us to own land, and we were like prisoners in our homeland.... We had not been able to perform our ceremonies, hold potlatches, or raise totem poles. We had been muted. (Davidson 2009, 2)

Previous broken promises and the pain of remembering the past kept the excitement from building until about one month before the pole raising. As my father explained, "About a month before the pole raising, *Naanii* and *Tsinii* started having meetings about how we're gonna raise the pole, and so the momentum started to gravitate towards the pole raising."

When it was time to make preparations for the pole raising, the Elders gathered at my great-grandparents' home to piece together their collective memories of how the traditional pole raising took place, along with the associated protocols. During these gatherings, the Elders also remembered the songs and dances that had nearly been lost during the Potlatch Ban. My father recorded some of these gatherings, and I have heard the voices of those Elders as they worked together to remember the songs and the dances that had come so close to being lost completely.

> *Naanii* put it out to invite the Elders to their house and there would be about 20 or 25 of them and they'd start talking about the old days and it was all in Haida. So I'd be sitting by Uncle Alfred or Uncle Victor, and they would interpret for me. And the stories that came out were on how the pole was to be raised. About two weeks before, after the meetings, they would have sing practice, and *Tsinii* would be leading the songs. *Tsinii* knew them all, he knew more songs than anybody there. And they all had Haida words or stories. It wasn't chants that are being sung today. *Naanii* said he knew a lot of songs, and she was

> always sorry she didn't learn more from him. See, he was a historian. He knew more than people knew he knew, but he didn't flaunt it. When the moment was right he would come out with the information. So, they just started to sing. And Amanda Edgars would remember some songs and that would tweak *Tsinii* remembering other songs, and that would tweak Hannah Parnell singing a song or Emily White, *Naanii*'s oldest sister, Eliza Abrahams. *Tsinii* would be singing and people would sing with him. Joe Weir would lead a song and they'd sing with him. So it was really like a ping pong. At the practice, they'd all have different songs. *Naanii* Selina came to a couple of them and sang several songs. And other people would just be inspired to sing. And so, it was just like coming alive again. All of a sudden there was a flurry of reconnecting with our spirituality through song.

My mother echoed my father's description of the Elders, who would come alive with the songs and dances at these gatherings, "[The Elders] would arrive, barely able to hobble, and as soon as the drumming and singing started they were up dancing joyfully. And the memories kept coming through…" (S. Davidson, personal communication, March 17, 2018).

During the meetings with the Elders, my father also learned that there were protocols and ceremonies connected with the traditional raising of the pole.

> The people were very, very concerned. That generation was very, very concerned that it had to be done right. And leading up to the pole raising day, there was a company doing some work, I can't remember what they were doing. I think it had to do with the DND [Department of National Defense] when they were putting in the communications [facility], what they call "the elephant pen." They had cranes there and they offered to raise the pole with a crane, a hydraulic crane. And I posed the question in the meeting and [the Elders] said, "No, we want to do it traditional." And so the stories came out. They would talk for hours. And every one of them had a bit of information. So they were *living* their history.

My father told me that during one of these meetings, his *naanii* taught him the dances she remembered. One of these dances was the K'awhlaa, which was a dance that was based on a traditional rite of passage.

> In the time before contact, when young Haida men would come of age, they would go into the forest to fast in order to find their spirit. When they returned, they were in a spirit state and required the help of a shaman to return to a human state. In the [K'awhlaa] dance, the young man in the spirit

state hides behind the blanket wearing a mask to represent this non-human state. He dances this way, revealing his spirit self momentarily for the first three verses of the song. Then for the final verse, the dancer removes his mask and exposes his true self (Davidson 2018, 97).

When my great-grandmother demonstrated the dance for my father, she was unable to express the spirit state without the use of a mask. To help with her transformation to the spirit state, she placed a paper bag over her head. Seeing his *naanii* dancing with a paper bag over her head inspired my father to create masks. He explained that *"Naanii* dancing the *K'awhlaa* with a brown paper bag was an inspiration for me to create masks because there was absolutely nothing left in Massett. Nothing." In 2009, my father, my stepmother Terri-Lynn, and my uncle Reg hosted a fortieth anniversary celebration for the pole raising. At the celebration, I sang the power song about losing our treasures while my father danced with the paper bag over his head. This performance was to remind us how far we have come.

Robert Davidson dancing with paper bag mask.

"In the final weeks leading up to the completion of the totem pole, there were many meetings of the community Elders and younger elected band councillors trying to agree on protocol and logistics for where and how to raise the pole and how to organize the subsequent celebration" (S. Davidson, personal communication, March 17, 2018). These conversations were complicated by the fact that Old Massett consisted of people from multiple separate villages, which meant there was no precedent for how to collaborate or legitimize rank and authority (*ibid*).

As the time for the pole raising approached, my father did not always know why it was so important for him to carve and raise the pole. In our conversations, he often spoke about having to keep going even though he did not know where he would end up. He had to trust that his intuition would guide him.

> I like to think about the potlatch, the feast as a creation. It's a canvas, and every idea is an intuitive message. Like I'm drawing on my intuition, but I may not know what that message is right away. So, when the totem pole was raised, I questioned, why am I doing this, during the process. And after several weeks of thinking that question, I said, "I'll find out later." And very shortly after that, you know, many of those old people died. So it was really closing that chapter of that generation. And before that chapter was closed, they volunteered their knowledge through the totem pole raising.

Today, my father's intuition is strengthened by his past experiences and practice, but when he was creating the pole, he had to trust that he was on the right path and watch for affirmations that this was true.

> When the pole was finally complete, the community's response began to shift. After I carved the totem pole, the momentum was really strong. I don't know how many blanket designs I made. I had requests, so I made five or six blanket designs. *Tsinii* had one already, a blanket, and *Naanii* gave it to me after he died. And Susan wore *Naanii*'s regalia. So some people had blankets.

In her biography[15], my great-grandmother described how she began to make button blankets again after the Potlatch Ban was lifted.

> After we lost our home in 1952 when we went fall fishing with my cousin Douglas, I bought material and pearl buttons from Eaton's in Vancouver so I could make a button blanket. I was the first person from Masset to make

---

15 Blackman, Margaret. *During My Time: Florence Edenshaw Davidson, a Haida Woman*. Seattle and London: University of Washington Press, 1982.

button blankets in recent years. I had no home so I wanted to do something. I made just one then, working on it for two years in my spare time. My husband drew a grizzly bear design for it. I kept it secret because I thought someone might laugh at me for doing such an old fashioned thing (Davidson, as cited in Blackman 1982, 124).

People were invited to the pole raising with invitations silkscreened by my father and a group of volunteers.

> The Village of Old Masset
>
> invites you to attend a
>
> Totem Pole Raising
>
> By the Eagle and Raven Clans.
>
> We would be proud to have you
>
> honour us with your presence,
>
> on 22 August 1969

They also silkscreened 600 prints to give out at the feast.

My father was only 22 years old when he carved the totem pole in 1969. I remember being incredibly aware of this achievement when I turned 22. Over the years, I have often wondered how he decided to do something so significant at such a young age. At 22, I was still trying desperately to find my way, so it was reassuring for me to learn that, despite how it may have appeared, he too had been trying to find his way. He did not really have a definitive plan when he began.

> Carving the totem pole, I never ever thought of not doing it. It never ever occurred to me. It didn't even enter my mind, I just knew I had to get to it. Like squaring off the back, I have no idea, I just had to do it. I was a smart alecky young kid coming in thinking I'm gonna teach the old folks something, but really I had nothing – all I had was the totem pole. And they gave it the depth through song and dance and the stories and history.

Connecting to sk'ad'a

My father's initial learning relied upon the strength of his relationships with his family and the Elders. In order for him to understand the information being shared at the Elder's meetings, he had to rely on his uncles to translate for him from Haida. He learned the dances from his *naanii*.

The totem pole project emerged out of my father's commitment to make a contribution to the Elders and his learning occurred through this contribution. His family acknowledged the strength required to complete this project by helping him to carve the pole and by encouraging him to continue. When he began the project, he did not know how to complete it, but he relied on the power of his mind to visualize the completed pole. This, along with his intuition, helped him as he worked toward raising the pole.

5
"That Pole Doesn't Belong to You Anymore"

> It was a wonderful day. It was the first time in [almost a century] that a totem pole had been raised in a Haida village. Everyone was so proud. The totems had all been cut down by the early missionaries. They thought we worshipped them. They didn't realize that they represented our written history. It seemed very fitting for the pole to stand in front of the very church that had been responsible for destroying our poles in those early years. (C. Davidson, n.d)

The pole was intended as a gift to the village, so it was placed in front of the Anglican church as that was considered to be a "neutral" location, in the sense that it was not connected to either the Raven or Eagle moiety or a particular family – which it would have been if it had been placed in front of someone's home. However, my father recognized that even this location posed certain complications.

> [The pole was put] in a neutral place in front of the church. It's kind of ironic, because it was the church that was part of ensuring that we were being removed from our cultural values, philosophies. Not a slap in the face to the church – that was not my intention. It was more because it was neutral ground. And there wasn't really any suitable place on the waterfront. And the majority of the Elders approved that site too.

Preparing to Raise the Pole

A potlatch, which included a large feast, was planned for all of the guests after the pole raising. According to Margaret Blackman (1977),

> Feasting was an element in the cycle of the Haida potlatch events, but feasting also occurred outside the context of the potlatch. While given on special occasions, such as the first naming of a child or a marriage, feasts were in

addition held for no other reason than to demonstrate one's wealth and position. A Haida Chief was expected to give frequent feasts, and in order to "keep the chief's place" which had been acquired through the potlatch, he was obliged to give a feast each winter. (41)

My great-grandmother was the head cook and was therefore responsible for ensuring that all of the guests were fed. Traditionally, food was used to legitimize Haida social positions and different foods were associated with different classes. To this day, as a sign of respect, guests are provided with food and refreshments whenever it is possible (Boelscher 1989). The preparation of the food for the potlatch required extensive planning long before the day of the pole raising. Because of Haida Gwaii's remote location, it also involved having items flown in from Vancouver.

> When [Robert] finished the pole we made a long list of food for the doing – half a side of beef, apples and oranges, grapefruit. The band councillors asked Robert if we could let the feast go and let them do it because we were old. I'm sorry now I let it go; we could have done it, but they asked us for it.

> I bought lots of towels, all kinds of cups, mugs, aprons, and nylons. We spent about a thousand dollars on little presents. Vivian [Robert's mother] spent about five hundred dollars on hers and Robert about six hundred dollars on towels and things. We weren't going to do it, but Phoebe and Charlotte Marks told me, "Florence, don't think too little of this doing. This is the biggest thing your grandson is going to do. You'll feel sorry afterwards when you think of it; all your life you'll feel bad over it. You're wise, but I want to give you advice." (Davidson, as cited in Blackman 1982, 131)

As the day of the pole raising approached, the Elders continued their meetings, demonstrating their commitment to raising the pole in the traditional way. Though none of them had been alive when the last pole raising had taken place, they continued to work together and shared stories to help one another remember how it had been done before.

> I could still hear *Tsinii* saying…that's the only part I could interpret, when he was describing how the totem pole was to be raised. He said, the person directing the pole raising, he said, "Ahhh-heee!" He'd go like that. It's when the pole moved. And every time the pole moved, they'd brace it up with the A-frame. And he's the one that directed us or directed people to have three different lengths of A-frame. The first one was very short, when the pole was first being lifted up. And then when the pole went up a little further, they had the

middle length up, and when it was three quarters of the way up they had the longer A-frames up. And that was to support it while the pullers were resting. And that's exactly how Dad did it, raised a pole. Ahhh-heee! And then the pole went up. So, I feel those meetings sparked a lot of other people's memories. Elijah Jones, Peter Hill, when they spoke, they all drew on historical experience or stories they heard. *Tsinii* never saw a totem pole being raised, but he drew on the stories from before.

Claude Davidson directs the raising of the pole.

My father elaborated on the significance of the sharing and the reinforcement of knowledge between the Elders who relied on their collective memory to ensure that the protocols were followed.

> None of them saw a pole raising, but they reassured each other with the stories they heard. Like when Lawrence Bell [my childhood friend] and I get together we talk about some of the values, and we confirm what we know about the values and our understanding of those values, and that's actually what happened at the meetings.

The pole was carved in front of my grandfather's house, but it was moved to the church the night before it was to be raised. This was a short distance down the road, so the community used cedar poles as rollers to move the pole.

> The night before [the pole raising], the pole was to be moved from Mom and Dad's house to the church. They had some cedar poles, two cedar poles and rollers. And a lot of people came out, I don't think we have a lot of photographs of that, but the long poles were like skids and the rollers were on top of that and the totem pole was rolled on those rollers. It rolled on the skids and people were pulling them. And as you pull it, the roller actually comes out the back and so someone from the back will rush around to put it in front again. And so you had to keep that momentum going. And I remember pulling with people and *Tsinii* was there directing and about twenty minutes into it, he poked me in the back. He said, "Robert, that pole doesn't belong to you anymore, it belongs to them" and so I stood back and let it go.

My father often speaks of letting art go once it has been completed, and I believe this idea emerged from his *tsinii*'s words so many years ago. I have never understood that the completion and subsequent letting go means that the art belongs to another individual once it has been completed; rather that the being that emerged from the wood or the canvas or the paper or the metal has been freed by its creator and can now be "let go" into the world. In the case of the pole in 1969, my father had to let it go, as it now belonged to the village. However, the experience and the knowledge that came from carving it has remained with my father over the years, and he attributes the depth of his understanding of Haida art to that first pole and the knowledge that came from the Elders.

My father believes that the energy of the pole in the village even impacted the weather.

> So having all that energy, the pulsating energy, actually cleared the sky. I really believe that. Because the day before, it was raining, and that evening we were moving the pole to the site, and the sky started opening up. The next day it was a beautiful day, the next day it was another beautiful day, and then it started raining again.

On the day of the pole raising, everything came together, although my father has no idea how it all happened.

> Robin Brown, he loaned his rope. Like there was all these things. Poles had to be gotten, I don't know who got them. The cedar poles, for the skids and for the A-frame. So all these things, someone was looking after it. *Tsinii* said, "You gotta get some rocks," and I don't know who got the rocks. But it was all there ready for the pole raising. So, when they came together, each one [had a bit of knowledge], that's where the notion came to me about being connected by a

thin thread 'cause when we all came together, they all had a bit of information and all of a sudden we have this thick rope.

My great-grandfather told my father that he also had to perform a ceremony before the pole was raised; this was to breathe "life into the pole in its new form and its new incarnation" (T. Williams-Davidson, personal communication, April 29, 2018).

Before [the pole was raised], *Tsinii* warned me, he said, "The head carver ties all the tools he used and drapes it around his neck before the pole is to be raised." And you do a little, he didn't call it a chant, he just said, "And you hah, hah, hah, hah, hah, hah, hah around the pole," and I was so shy to do that that I pretended to forget. But Uncle Victor was MC, and I guess *Tsinii* got him to call me and told him I had to do the chant first, so I went rushing to find the tools I had used, tied them up and did that chant. And it felt so amazing to do that, like to holler around the pole, the totem pole.

Robert Davidson Sr. coaches Robert for the carvers' chant in Haida.

My *tsinii* was so proud of my father's achievement, "It was a very exciting day. Robert [chanted] around the pole with his face painted and carrying his carving tools. It was a proud moment for me and especially for my dad [Robert Davidson, Sr.] and all the family" (Davidson, n. d.).

To honour the commitment to raise the pole in a traditional way, ropes were attached to the pole and three A-frames of increasing sizes were used to push the pole up into position, just as my great-grandfather had described in the meetings.

> Nobody witnessed a totem pole raising in Massett. *Tsinii* was 89. I asked *Naanii* if any were raised in Masset, and she said no. But *Tsinii* understood, and he's the one that orchestrated the A-frames that were used. And also, he asked people to have rocks for when the pole was being buried and that would encourage drainage, prolong the life of the tree, the totem pole. And then [they] also dug the trench down. There were four ropes: two to pull and two to balance it. And Dad, your *tsinii*, he took on the job of directing the pullers.

My grandfather directed the raising of the pole according to the instructions that were conveyed to him by my great-grandfather.

> We tied ropes on the top of the pole and the whole village pulled the ropes until the pole was raised. We had an A-frame brace that we placed under the pole and the whole village pulled it up. I would shout, "Heave[16]!" and everyone would pull. It took one hour of pulling and finally the pole was in place. (Davidson, n. d.)

Raising the pole.

---

16 When my grandfather described this process, he used the word "heave" which may have been due to the public's unfamiliarity with the traditional practice described by his father.

My parents explained that the pole did not have to be adjusted after it was raised, that somehow, it just turned around to face the correct direction as it was raised. My father said that "it was amazing because the pole was actually facing like that [demonstrates with hands], and as it was going up it actually turned. We didn't turn it. It just automatically turned to where it's facing." I understood this to be a positive affirmation from the ancestors for the events of the day. My father believed it was evidence that they had tapped into a higher power, like they were all being looked after.

Once the pole had been raised, the crowd cheered and the singing began.

> There was sure a lot of happy people that day. It did that and more. It actually triggered [an opening] up to our spirituality. It opened up to ceremony. It gave strength to relearning our songs and dances. It gave reason to sing our songs again.

The pole raising was followed by a potlatch in the community hall. According to my *tsinii*, my great-grandmother made "huge pots of stew and the tables were laden with fruit, pies, cakes, and biscuits. The family handed out potlatch gifts depicting a Raven-Eagle design silk-screened on both cloth and paper." People from New Masset, Hydaburg, Skidegate, and Vancouver all attended the potlatch.

> All the dignitaries of New Masset were invited, there was a group from Skidegate, a group from Hydaburg. And the Skidegate people did some songs, *Naanii* and *Tsinnii* did some songs, Amanda Edgars, and some songs were done by Hydaburg. And April Churchill, she was doing ballet then, and she did one dance. They didn't really have a PA system, so I don't really know what *Tsinii* talked about, but he spoke. Everything was in Haida. And they had a group of people dancing. And at the same time, I'm not sure what the timing was, I presented the totem pole to the village. And Eugene Samuels was the Chief Councillor then who accepted the pole on behalf of the village. And everything took place in the old community hall. I think it accommodated 400-500 people.

Though it is common to invite people from New Masset and Hydaburg to events today, it was much rarer in 1969.

> It was a real big deal, I felt. Hydaburg came over, the powers that be in New Masset came, the town mayor, New Masset mayor, and it was a real big deal in those days when the white folks were part of our celebration.

Over the months that my father carved the pole and even during the pole raising and the potlatch, he did not always know why he was raising the pole, but he always knew that he had to continue with what he was doing.

> You know, when I look back. There were many times I questioned myself, why am I doing this? 'Cause there was so much turmoil. But mostly good. The people wanted blanket designs and the songs were being sung again. And *Tsinii* and *Naanii*, you know, like they weren't young, but they were busy hosting and fortunately, the aunties would help. They would all do the cooking and baking for refreshments.

In 2009, for the fortieth anniversary of the pole raising, my father created a book filled with photographs from the day. These photographs capture the memories of the event while also demonstrating the re-emergence of our art and our cultural expressions after a long period of forced dormancy. In some images, there are head pieces made from cardboard and tissue paper with feathers that are dyed vibrant colours. During one of our conversations, my father flipped through the pages of this book. He was particularly saddened to see the toy drum that my great-grandfather held in his hands.

> I sure was sad when I saw [the toy drum]. I mean you know, just to show how far we've gone. There were only three drums that day. That's one. A toy drum. And the headpieces. [They were] just painted on a piece of wood.

Robert Davidson Sr. with toy drum.

"That Pole Doesn't Belong to You Anymore" | **53**

My father's voice changed as he showed me the photograph. I, too, understood that this image provided a glimpse of how far we have come, and I appreciated my father's continued ability to focus on our strength.

Connecting to *sK'ada*

To prepare for the pole raising, the Elders pieced together fragments of their history and the stories that they had preserved to collectively remember the protocols. They were committed to honouring these aspects of spirituality and protocol in the raising of the pole. They brought a cultural depth to the pole raising that my father had not anticipated, and this experience inspired my father to further explore the connection between traditional ceremony and the art form.

6

Born "in the Nick of Time"

My father says that his generation was born "in the nick of time." There was so much knowledge that lived with the Elders, and many of those Elders passed away shortly after the pole raising in 1969. I have always believed that they waited to ensure their knowledge would continue to live, and the threads they held would continue to thicken the rope even after they were gone. I asked my father if he thought that his *tsinii* had waited, and my father responded, "He did. He [waited]. Auntie Emily told me, she said after the pole was raised, she found [*Tsinii*] lying on the couch, and he said, "My job is done. I saw my grandson raise the pole." Three weeks later, my great-grandfather passed away. If he did wait, he was correct in his belief that my father understood enough about Haida ceremony to host future potlatches and feasts so that our ceremonial practices would continue to be passed on.

After the pole raising in 1969, the second potlatch that my father attended was in 1976, hosted by Chief *Gaalaa*. As my father explained, every other event he had attended prior to that would have been considered a feast, whether it was a Christmas dinner, a picnic, or a wedding supper. However, despite their apparent disconnection from ceremony, those events had been used by the Elders to "solidify their history with one another."

When Chief *Gaalaa* became chief, my father said that he was "scratching the bottom on songs." He remembered that my uncle Reg was really excited about dancing and asked my father to "sing another one." My father admitted that, at the time, he only knew four Haida songs, so he had to tell his brother he had already sung all of the songs that he knew.

To learn the songs, my father listened to the old tapes that had been recorded in preparation for the pole raising of 1969 and practiced them with his *naanii*.

I would listen to those tapes over and over and over and over and over again. Eventually, I started to sing them. And eventually I would sing them in front of *Naanii*, and she would explain to me what they meant and correct my pronunciation.

When my father described this process, I recognized it immediately because he had used the same method to teach me the songs.

Charles Edenshaw Memorial Longhouse Feast (1978)

In 1976, Parks Canada commissioned my father to create a memorial longhouse to honour his great-grandfather Charles Edenshaw's contribution to Canadian art. The memorial longhouse included a carved house front and four house posts that were completed in 1978. Then there was an official ceremony to dedicate the memorial to Charles Edenshaw and to raise the house posts (Stewart 1979). As the event approached, my father began to wonder about the kinds of songs that should be sung on such an occasion.

Florence Davidson in front of the Edenshaw Longhouse.

> There was a celebration in the village to honour the completion of the Edenshaw Memorial. So that tweaked more curiosity about what songs do we sing here to honour this moment? And it was like primary school, like there was so many people wanting to know more and wanting to sing more and dance.

As the Haida Gwaii Singers Society (2008) explains,

> There are many different kinds of songs, each for specific uses. Certain songs are brought out in a specific order depending upon the formality of an event. Sometimes the beginning singers sing songs that are inappropriate for certain occasions. Song protocol as it has come to be called, is the set of rules about when certain songs may be used and what kind of dance or ceremony accompanies a song. It also encompasses who may use certain songs and the need to obtain permission to sing songs and to acknowledge song owners and teachers. (9)

The importance of honouring the protocols associated with Haida art were deeply ingrained in my father, my uncle, and my *tsinii*. In 1978, when my father had finished carving the four house posts for the Charles Edenshaw Memorial, he wanted to honour the eight apprentices who had assisted him, with a feast. The event was planned to occur on the Saturday, and my father, uncle, and *tsinii* got word on Friday that it had not been organized.

> I thought it would be a good idea to honour the eight apprentices, so I organized with the band manager a feast to honour them. We set a date. [Dad, Reg, and I] were fishing at the Yakoun River then. It was going to happen on the Saturday and we got word Friday night that they weren't going to do it. Nothing was organized and people were flying [up] from Vancouver for the event. But the three of us organized it at the Yakoun River. Dad, Reg, and I. We took the salmon from the smokehouse, went to the village, by noon we had all the invitations out. We just knew it had to be done. I think two people didn't show up, there were 71 invited, 69 showed up.

As my father's knowledge of Haida ceremony expanded, so did his commitment to ensuring our traditional practices continued to thrive. He felt that his experiences helped him to identify the themes for each of the potlatches and feasts that he hosted over the years. As my father explained his understanding of his own process, I began to understand more about how, with each feast or potlatch[17], he was working to fill a void that he saw in our cultural knowledge, a void that inhibited our ability to continue to share our ancestral knowledge.

---

[17] For a complete list of the potlatches and feasts that my father hosted and co-hosted, see Appendix A.

Tribute to the Living Haida Feast (1980)

The inspiration for the Tribute to the Living Haida came from the observation that we need to honour life.

> The Tribute to the Living Haida was to make a statement, it's okay to honour the living. But in retrospect, [I realize] the reason why we didn't honour the present was because of the laws that governed us and the children being taken away from the families and breaking up the families and losing our connections to our spirituality, losing our connection to the land.

As with the Elders' meetings so many years before, my father found that when he hosted this feast, it triggered more memories of the old ways. Remembering how he had watched his *naanii* dance with the paper bag, my father decided to carve a K'awhlaa mask for the potlatch. Following the dance performance with that mask, he was provided with additional information about how the mask should look.

> When we danced [the K'awhlaa], Adam Bell gave me more information on how the mask should be. He said, "That mask should have Eagle feathers on it." So all these things were tweaking people's memory, just by demonstrating it. And it was really a shot in the dark for me, doing all these things.

My father was still early in his learning, and he made mistakes. Because saving face in Haida culture is very important, it was crucial to make things right when these mistakes were made. However, it was difficult to make things right after the fact if he was not informed of mistakes during the event.

> Doing the four-day feast…I upset a few people on how I conducted it. But that was also a learning curve for me. I remember a couple [of people] bawling me out. I said, "I would rather you tell me at the time so I can rectify it, not after it happened."

Children of the Good People (1981)

My father's inspiration to host his first potlatch came about when he decided to adopt Nuu-Chah-Nulth artist, Joe David. In order to host the potlatch, my father had to return once again to his family for guidance. He explained to me that at that time "there was a lot of regret that we [were] losing our Haida names," so he decided to invite families to give names to their children and grandchildren at the potlatch.

That's when I talked with Uncle Alfred to give [the potlatch] a name. He gave me the name Children of the Good People because this was a forum for names to be given to the children and grandchildren because in order for [naming] to happen, it had to be in a public forum.

Susan Davidson with her children Sara and Ben.

In preparation for this potlatch, my great-grandmother sent my father to talk to Elders from the village; she also asked Elder Dora Brooks to accompany my father to translate for him, as all of the Elders spoke Haida.

> [*Naanii*] directed me. Go talk to Emily Abrahams, go talk to Amanda Edgars, go talk to Adam Bell, go talk with Grace Wilson, go talk with…and so on. And I would talk with them and share my ideas with them. And Uncle Alfred too, Uncle Victor. And they would give me insights and that helped me to plan the first [four-day] feast. I asked if it was okay to record them. I recorded some of them. And some didn't want to be recorded, so I would let them know what the potlatch was for and then invited them to give names. It was to give names to the children. And because it was a two-day event, I chose to have the Ravens first and then the Eagles the second day. And there was some resistance to that.

Reflecting on his *naanii*'s direction now, my father believes that at the time, she was mentoring him to develop allies.

> When I look back now, it was more like creating allies. Because when I presented the idea, they would fine tune it for me, "If you did it this way, then… it's okay" "I don't think it's a good idea if you did that…"

End of Mourning Ceremony. In the summer of 1981, as my father prepared to host the potlatch, the Charles Edenshaw Memorial longhouse burned down.

> The longhouse burned down at the same time I was planning for the potlatch, and it was a real blow to myself and the village to have it burn down. And I remember coming home to Whonnock and singing a crying song. I said, "Okay we're always lamenting something. There's no end to lamenting." So that's when I decided to seek guidance from *Naanii* and *Naanii* Selina. [I asked them], "Is it okay to do a ceremony to end the mourning of the longhouse?" And I presented the idea to them, and they said, "Yeah, that sounds okay." And that idea came from other experiences. It's not something that I made up.

This idea for a ceremony to end the mourning evolved into a black frog dance that my uncle performed at the potlatch. My father chose the frog to represent the memorial longhouse because the design on the house front, adapted from a Charles Edenshaw chief seat, had included a frog. The black frog dance is one of my most vivid memories from that potlatch, and I have never witnessed a dance like it since that day. However, that dance was not one that had been performed before that time, and my father had to go through the process of seeking permission from the Elders to introduce such a ceremony.

> The idea, after the longhouse burned down, was to sing a power song. Then, I asked Reg to carve a black frog mask, and he danced the frog. And I had this Eagle Spirit mask, and so Joe David danced that after the frog dance because I felt we had to have a balance [which was provided by the red Eagle Spirit mask]. And later that evening, with the frog dance, we just changed one word from "*I* lost all my treasures" to "*We* lost all our treasures," and I said, "Is this okay?" to *Naanii* Selina, and she said, "That sounds good." So, we did the dance at my potlatch and later on that evening, we built a bonfire at Reggie's house and sang songs, and I burned the frog mask. And that symbolized the end of mourning. And that gave birth to the end of mourning ceremony. Because I feel we need to mark the end of mourning, acknowledge the end of mourning, so we can move on.

The reason for burning the mask was to mark the end of the mourning period for the loss of the longhouse. As my father explained, "We carry the pain, and we have to symbolically choose a time to end that pain." It is my understanding that if this end is not marked, we will continue to mourn those losses, which will weaken our spirits.

In 1986, there was a memorial for my great-uncle Alfred and my great-aunt Rose, and my father decided to further expand on the idea of the end of mourning ceremony. Once again, he sought permission from the Elders to perform this ceremony. My father emphasized that it was very important for him to ensure that people supported what he did.

> I made portrait masks of my aunt and uncle to bring them back from the spirit world, and it worked. People were stunned, they were magnetized by the images. It was eerie, as though they really had come back. The masks brought to mind incomplete ideas and thoughts about those people, and bringing them back one more time helped us to complete our life with them, so that we could let them go. People responded by saying that they hadn't seen that mourning ceremony for a long time. (Davidson & Steltzer 1994, 98–99)

What was particularly compelling about many of these "new" ceremonies, is that the Elders remembered them, even though they had not been performed during their lifetimes.

Payment. Traditionally, the Haida gave payments to guests who witnessed the potlatch. Today, many people refer to these payments as gifts. Historically, there were strict protocols associated with the payment that the guests received. For example, if you were an Eagle attending a Raven potlatch, you would be paid, but if you were a Raven attending a Raven potlatch, you would not be paid.

> Today, everybody gets the payment. Traditionally they were called payments. You're paying your guests for the service of witnessing. And today they call them gifts, but I feel it's almost too far ingrained. Can we change? Is it important to go back to those old values of the opposite Clan being paid? Because my understanding is you never pay yourself. Like I don't pay the Eagles. For example one of the payments I made were 24 drums that I made, two dozen drums because there were no drums in the village, and I remember several people saying, "Oh, I'd sing a song, but I don't have a drum." So I gave those out. And also I made bracelets. And it seems kind of funny in today's way of thinking, but the bracelets went to my aunties, my s<u>k</u>aan. So I think that's another level of thinking that I feel is important to relearn. Like my s<u>k</u>aan, the

women of my dad's [Raven] Clan, were great. They made great contributions to my potlatch, so that was my payment to them. See in the Anglo way of thinking, it's *all* the women, whether you're Eagle or Raven, who are your aunties. But in Haida way, all the women of my dad's Clan, are my aunties, my *skaan*. So, I don't know how many people understood that. Like how I organized the potlatch, was through the information that I got through the different Elders, Adam Bell, Emily Abrahams, Dora Brooks, people like that. Amanda Edgars, *Naanii*, Uncle Victor, Uncle Alfred, so I would pass it by them first. Okay, this is what I want to do, and if there was any offence to that, they would ask, "Could you do it this way?" So they were fine tuning my ideas. And the ideas came from the information from the old folks.

Every Year the Salmon Come Back (1989)

My father was brought up to demonstrate gratitude for the food that he received from the land and the water, and he was taught to treat animals with respect. The idea for the Every Year the Salmon Come Back feast was to publicly demonstrate this gratitude for the annual return of the sockeye.

> I had a two day feast in Massett, and that was to give thanks for the return of the salmon. [I called it] Every Year the Salmon Come Back because I would privately, leading up to that two-day feast, I would privately, mentally thank the river as I was leaving it for giving up, the fish, for the salmon. I would thank the salmon, thank the forest, and just have gratitude for the abundance.

To honour the salmon, my father composed a song and collaborated with my uncle Reg to create a dance. However, my father does not take credit for the song and the dance in the way one might expect. Instead, he attributes these inspirations to his ability to connect with our cosmic memory, a term that he has borrowed, which refers to our ability to "tap into something greater" than ourselves and our own knowledge.

> When the Rainbow Creek [Dancers] introduced the Salmon Dance, one of the Elders said, "Wow! I haven't seen that dance for a long time." So I feel we have this cosmic memory and [he snaps his fingers] ideas are already there. So when we're fluent in that medium then we're open to inspiration in drawing the ideas from that cosmic whatever, wherever those ideas are and however they are stored. It's like being a radio transistor, you turn the dial and, "Oh wow, I like that classical music" or "I like this folk music," so you become finely tuned. My creativity comes from that, from the foundation of the old masters.

During that feast, my father also adopted Judson Brown.

> I made really good friends with a Tlingit Elder, Judson Brown; he adopted me into his Clan. His Clan gave me a name *hintaach*, the sound the killer whale makes as it dives. And to reciprocate that, I adopted him in 1989.

The main theme for this feast was to demonstrate gratitude for the abundance that we have; for this reason, my father connected this theme to his art and the contribution he could make to his home community.

> I had the idea to show gratitude for the abundance we were born into. The salmon, every year the salmon come back, the art, the land, our culture. And also, to continue the gifting, I presented the village with one of my bronze killer whales. Just to keep me in good standing, I guess. It's giving back. When I gave them the large sculpture, "Meeting and the Centre," they said, "How come you're giving it to us?" I said, "Well, I really like what's going on here. You've created a lot of totem poles, and I want to be part of it."

Memorial for Arlene Nelson and Arnold Davidson (1992)

In 1992, my father and my uncle hosted a memorial potlatch for their sister Arlene and their brother Arnold. Because of my father and his siblings being Eagles, this was considered an Eagle potlatch. While preparing for this potlatch, my father and my uncle decided to try to bring back the old way of paying the opposite Clan for witnessing the potlatch. In this case, it would mean that only the Ravens were paid for their attendance. They decided the best way to do this was to give ribbons to the people who belonged to the Raven Clans. My father explained that it was not his intention to go back to the old ways, rather it was to "shine a light on what it used to be like or how it was in the old days."

Urban Feasts (1993/1994)

Historically, Haida potlatches and feasts took place on traditional Haida territory, but in 1993 and 1994, my father decided to host feasts, which he called Urban Feasts, in Vancouver. The idea to host a Haida feast in an urban setting emerged from his recognition that there are many Haida people who do not live on Haida Gwaii. In fact there is such a large urban population of Haida people that the Council of the Haida Nation, our national government, has regional representation in Vancouver. My father was familiar with the challenges of living away from his homeland and working to remain connected to our ancestral and cultural knowledge, and for this reason, he decided to host the Urban Feasts. He hoped that these feasts would bring Haida culture to the urban setting. These feasts were two-day events, and my father laughed as he explained why the two days were necessary.

> I jokingly said the first day is for us to get to know each other 'cause I remember one person saying, "Wow, I haven't seen you for 50 years!" Just comments like that. And I jokingly said, "We'll get to know each other the first day and the second day we'll fall in love." And it was really another learning curve for me.

Gyaa 'isdlaa (2016)

The idea for the *gyaa 'isdlaa* emerged from a memorial that my father attended. As he explained, "I was at a memorial, and this person, they had stuff hanging in the hall that had nothing to do with his crest, and that's when I decided to give each Clan a dance screen with their crest." My father understood that this oversight was a result of the loss of our cultural knowledge. He has always felt that it is important to build a stronger foundation of that cultural knowledge. The *gyaa 'isdlaa* was intended to serve that purpose by honouring the surviving Haida Clans of Haida Gwaii.

> The [*gyaa 'isdlaa*] was to shine a light on all the sub-crests of each Clan. And also to mention their Haida name of their Clan, and so they all recognize what Clan they belong to. So, I feel that's a good start.

To ensure that the community understood what he was hoping to achieve with the *gyaa 'isdlaa,* my father held meetings with his Clan in the village. These meetings gave the Clan members an opportunity to participate in organizing the agenda for the events and to voice any concerns that they had.

> I hosted three or four meetings to explain what my plans were. And the other part of it is, I did explain that at the potlatch my payment will be the dance screens. So the Clan will receive the dance screen, and it's not for sale. I did say that. It's an identification marker for when that Clan hosts, and I am excited to see that they are using them.

It is important to involve the members of the Clan for organizational purposes. Furthermore

> Calling in one's lineage mates and elders of related or otherwise important lineages manifests the respect one has for them; it demonstrates the host's

willingness to "listen to your elders" and "take advice from your people," both of which are considered necessary to maintain public esteem. (Boelscher 1989, 80)

Redistribution of Knowledge

It is important to emphasize that the feasts and potlatches that my father hosted and co-hosted were not for the purpose of making his name better or increasing his personal status. They were for the purpose of sharing his understanding with the community and to encourage more learning about our community's collective knowledge. As he said so many times throughout our conversations, hosting and co-hosting these doings was a significant learning process for him. My father is very committed to sharing his knowledge, and he has often spoken to me about the importance of being generous with what we know.

I believe that is what he was hoping to achieve with that first pole raising – to share the knowledge that he had gained from the Elders. Though I recognize that there are protocols associated with some knowledge, it is important to share what we can so that we may all benefit. Furthermore, our potential for growth is directly connected to our ability to innovate as times change and new situations emerge.

Before the *gyaa 'isdlaa*, I had an idea to publicly acknowledge that my dissertation research did not belong only to me – that the knowledge emerging from my research belonged to the community. I presented this idea of introducing a new tradition to my father, and he thought it was a good idea. With his support, I presented canvas photographs of a Dogfish Mother, which was created by my brother, to key representatives from community and organizations who were in attendance at the *gyaa 'isdlaa*. I did this to publicly acknowledge that my dissertation research was not solely my own. Through new practices such as this one, we will continue to expand and add depth to our knowledge.

Connecting to sk̲'ad'a

My father's learning process has been guided by his own curiosity about our history and his ability to take account of what was lost. His willingness to make contributions to our knowledge through the hosting of feasts and potlatches has resulted in a greater knowledge and understanding of our history, at the same time reaffirming our commitment to honouring our protocols.

His learning emerged from the strong relationships he has with his family and his community, and it resulted in the commitment to provide authentic experiences that fostered learning and teaching of our ancient knowledge in our community.

7

Potlatch as Pedagogy

The first time I recognized the potlatch was being used as pedagogy was at the *gyaa 'isdlaa* in 2016. I had recently completed my PhD in education, and my eyes could only see the world through a lens of learning. As I witnessed the *gyaa 'isdlaa*, I was able to understand for the first time how the Haida potlatch was being used as a tool to relearn and reteach ceremony. My father had relearned ceremonial knowledge from the Elders in preparation for the pole raising, and he was now using the potlatch as a means of sharing what he had learned about our ancestral knowledge with our community. However, my own understanding of my father's achievement emerged from my observations as an educator, so I asked him if it had been his intention to teach about ceremony and protocol through the potlatch.

> When I look back, it certainly has that feeling. But I don't claim that, I think it has to come from someone else. But I know in terms of ceremony, it certainly helped me to understand the art form. Like up to that point, the art was really a commodity for me – and the fact that the Elders responded in the way that they did gave it more credence. I didn't realize how important ceremony was until that event happened. I didn't realize how serious it was, especially to have *Naanii* and *Tsinii* host the several meetings at their house. Inviting all the old people in the village to express their opinion on how to conduct the day. It was really all the old people, the Elders coming together that was the recipe for the day, the agenda.

My father follows his intuition, but my mind operates in frameworks. My knowledge needs to be attached to a solid structure that can support it to expand and grow. As I reflected on the ways in which my father had used the potlatch as a form of pedagogy I realized, that without knowing it or intending to, he had used the *sk̲'ad'a* principles to teach us about Haida ancestral knowledge. Through the preparation and hosting of potlatches and feasts, he had demonstrated that learning emerges from strong relationships, authentic experiences, and from curiosity; that learning occurs through observation, contribution, and recognizing and encouraging strengths; and that learning honours the power of the mind, our history and our stories, as well as spirituality and protocol.

Learning Emerges from Strong Relationships

My father's learning about the protocols associated with the traditional pole raising relied upon his relationships. Even his initial understanding of the information being shared at the Elders' meetings relied upon his connections with his uncles Victor and Alfred who were able to translate the knowledge from Haida to English. Later, when he was preparing to host his own potlatches, his learning relied upon his ability to create strong allies. His relationship with his *naanii* allowed her to guide him in establishing these allies; she also taught him the songs and dances that were vital components of the potlatches and feasts.

As an educator, I know that my students' learning relies upon my ability to develop strong relationships, and that without those relationships, meaningful learning is unlikely to occur. My first priority is always to develop strong and respectful relationships with my students. Though I have not always been successful, it remains essential to me to continue to work at developing and strengthening those relationships. Strong relationships are particularly important when students are struggling in school because they need to be able to trust educators enough to allow them to provide support.

Learning Emerges from Authentic Experiences

In the stories my father told, he learned from authentic experiences, and he attributed his learning to the experience of hosting the potlatches and feasts.

> *Naanii* and *Tsinii*'s generation, they were the last generation [connected] to that ancient past, and I feel so lucky that I was able to relearn some of that. I don't speak Haida, but hosting the feasts and the potlatches, it was a learning exercise for me. I wouldn't have gained the insights if I'd just intellectualized about it. So actually going through the process. Sure I may have wrinkled a few people along the way, but that is the learning curve for me, to rectify it.

My father did not place much value on the intellectualizing aspects of his cultural experiences, but I believe these aspects did play a role in his learning.

However, "going through the process" had more of an impact on him because the theoretical knowledge became immediately applicable to a specific activity; it was not shared in isolation of the activity. The act of hosting a potlatch or feast provided a medium through which he could immediately demonstrate his learning and receive immediate feedback. Dancing the K̲'awhlaa mask gave my father the opportunity to learn more about the mask's historical attributes. Creating the mask provided the opportunity to share what he had learned, and dancing the mask in a public forum provided the opportunity for immediate feedback. In this way, the learning was embedded in the activity.

I am often asked about the term *authentic*, as some people struggle with the word. In response, I explain that authentic learning experiences often take place outside of the classroom; however, this is not a requirement. Rather, the learning must be *applicable* to the students' lives outside of school. When students learn from these authentic experiences, it also reinforces the importance of what they are learning. The sole purpose for learning something new should not be to "do better in school." Formal education can lose its meaning for many students when it does not allow them to imagine themselves in the worlds they inhabit outside of school.

Learning Emerges from Curiosity

My father's learning about ceremony and protocol emerged from the questions that he asked. This curiosity helped him to gather information when he wondered which songs to sing at the opening of the Charles Edenshaw Memorial Longhouse or whether or not he could introduce the end of mourning ceremony at his potlatch. Though my father continues to have questions, he must now seek his own answers to these questions. The Elders who were once there to guide him are now gone, and he must ask his family and friends or seek the guidance in books that have been written about our old ways. He firmly believes that he learned so much about Haida ceremony and protocol because of the questions he asked. Furthermore, he recognizes that it was through his ability to ask for help that he was able to learn from his grandparents and other Elders.

> In order to really honour our past [I needed] to ask questions on how to conduct a feast, how to conduct a potlatch. And that's one of the lessons I learned from *Naanii* was to ask so and so, go talk to so and so. Uncle Alfred, he was always a good guide, Uncle Victor, Dad. So I feel telling these stories [here] will add depth to my efforts.

I am sure it is not lost on my father that my own curiosity has prompted all of my questions, and it is a testament to his commitment to sharing his knowledge that he has never once become impatient and said, "*jaa 'aayaa*." The conversations have never been cut short, and perhaps this is his way of telling me that these are questions that need to be asked.

As educators, we often feel pressure to have all of the answers. As a result, we may guide our students to ask questions that align with our knowledge. But we do not need to have all of the answers. We can model curiosity for our students. We can seek answers to our own questions and teach students how to be comfortable with their curiosity and to find answers for themselves. Sometimes, the answers will not be known. In those moments, we can improvise based upon the knowledge we do have. We can also seek guidance in the same way that my father sought guidance so long ago, and the way he continues to seek guidance today.

Learning Occurs through Observation

My father observed gaps in our knowledge and understanding, and this awareness led him to host and co-host the feasts and potlatches. The understanding of these gaps guided the knowledge he sought, and his ability to learn through observation guided this learning.

When my great-grandmother taught my father how to dance the K'awhlaa, she did it by dancing the K'awhlaa, and he learned through watching her. His understanding of how he had learned through observation guided his thinking about how he might teach others through observation.

> All that I've learned is through demonstration. I've hired outside [dance] groups so that they could share with us where they're at through their song and dance. In 1981, I hired the *K'san* Dancers and they danced for us and that helped, so other people could witness where they're at with their song and dance. And with the *gyaa 'isdlaa* I hired Calvin Hunt and his group, and they danced for us and demonstrated where they're at through their song and dance. In Vancouver when I hosted the urban feasts, I did the same again. I hired outside groups so that they could share where they're at.

In this way, my father helped others to learn through observation.

Observation takes time. If we learn in this way, it will be a while before we are comfortable sharing what we understand. Therefore, we need to make time for learning through observation and honour the time that it takes for new understandings to emerge. Sometimes, it means we need to provide opportunities for our students to observe new skills before trying them independently. Sometimes, it means we need to slow down in our teaching to make space to support engagement with new topics.

Learning Occurs through Contribution

In his teachings, my father has always emphasized the importance of making a contribution; he does this through hosting feasts and potlatches, mentoring emerging artists, and sharing the knowledge that he has gained through his experiences. The significance of contribution was a recurring theme throughout all of our conversations. My father understood that carving the pole was a way to contribute to the community. Later, the potlatches and feasts that he hosted and co-hosted were his way of making a contribution. The knowledge that he gathered in preparation for these feasts and potlatches was shared publicly and contributed by strengthening our connection to our ancestors. His art was also a contribution. It began with a pole, and throughout the years, my father has given bronze and aluminum sculptures back to the village in acknowledgement of the strength and inspiration that he continues to draw from his community. Though these examples of contribution differ from fishing for halibut with his *tsinii*, the significance of making a contribution remains the same.

There are two aspects of the principle, "learning occurs through contribution." The first is how important learning becomes if we are learning for the purpose of contributing. If your family's supper is reliant upon your ability to catch a salmon, then you are going to be very motivated to learn to fish. The second involves recognizing the importance of making contributions in our culture. My father learned from the Elders for the purpose of sharing his knowledge, just as I pursued my education because I wanted to be able to contribute to my community through what I learned at school. In each of these examples, the learning emerged through a motivation to make a contribution to the community. In other words, it may be difficult to make learning relevant for Haida students if what is being taught does not lead to the ability to make a contribution to their family and community. This commitment to community and family as opposed to the individual is a way of being that has been carried forward from our past and is often misunderstood by educators who have been trained in mainstream educational institutions.

Learning Occurs Through Recognizing and Encouraging Strengths

My father recalled that my great-grandfather came to help him carve the pole, even though he was 89 years old. He recognized that this was my great-grandfather's way of encouraging him in his work. This was my great-grandfather's way of recognizing my father's ability to carve. My great-grandmother saw my father's potential as a liaison between the old people's knowledge and future generations, so she sent my father to talk to them. This was her way of acknowledging and encouraging my father's strength to bring together the old ways and the ways of today.

We can do this with our students as well. It is easy to point out what they are doing wrong, but how many times do we remember to acknowledge their strengths and their successes? We can take the time to get to know the students in our lives well enough to recognize and encourage their strengths. We can provide them with opportunities to share their strengths with others, so that their strengths are developed further.

Learning Honours the Power of the Mind

My father began carving the pole with only an idea and the vision that he would complete it. Throughout our conversations he also referenced his commitment to visualizing the outcome with regard to the potlatches and the feasts. In this way, he honoured the power of his mind to guide him. His ability to trust his vision was nurtured by his family, who reinforced and encouraged his strength.

In schools, we must reinforce and encourage students' strengths so that they too can use the power of their minds to successfully achieve what they set out to do. They must be able to see themselves as successful so they can accomplish these outcomes for themselves. As educators, we also need to support our students to strengthen their minds against adversity and continue to visualize a positive outcome for themselves.

Learning Honours History and Story

We have access to much of our knowledge today because our history and stories were kept alive through picnics, Christmas dinners, and weddings. Fragments of knowledge were pieced together to form a mosaic of narratives that taught us and connected us to our past. This knowledge is the reason we can still sing our old songs. This knowledge is the reason we can still dance our old dances. This knowledge is the reason we still know how to feast and potlatch.

In the classroom, I also use stories to teach. The narratives I share have the power to build connections between my students and me, and I always encourage other educators to share parts of themselves that they are comfortable sharing, by telling the stories of their lives. In my experience, it rarely works to formally teach a teenager about life. On the other hand, they will often listen to my stories and occasionally enjoy a laugh at the expense of my much younger and less wise self.

We can also follow appropriate protocols to incorporate traditional Indigenous stories into our classes. This provides students with different perspectives on the role and use of stories while introducing them to diverse story arcs. I am consistently amazed by the power of stories to connect me with the generations that came before me, as well as with present and future generations.

Learning Honours Aspects of Spirituality and Protocol

My father explained that in 1969 all he had to contribute was the pole, and it was the Elders who brought the pole to life through their old knowledge. He said that the depth of the knowledge emerged through the ceremony they brought to the pole.

When we share our knowledge, there is no separation between the spiritual realm and the one in which we live. With his chant around the pole, my father breathed life into the pole – as a living being, his equal. My great-grandfather spoke to the halibut like a person; there was no distinction between the human and the animal worlds. The end of mourning ceremony allows us to visit our loved ones one more time after they are gone.

Though it may not always be appropriate to share ceremonial knowledge publicly in a school setting, we need to recognize that this spiritual knowledge is a significant aspect of the knowledge that our students bring with them from their homes and communities to school. We need to ensure that we do not undermine that knowledge with our teaching. Spiritual understandings may significantly contribute to our students' identities, and they need to be honoured and respected.

The Paper Bag

The Potlatch Ban severely impacted our ability to use the potlatch to reinforce our identity and culture as Haida people. Our Elders managed to preserve some of the knowledge to share with future generations, but so much of it was lost. Those Elders, who my father used to seek out for guidance, are now gone. My father recognizes that it is now his generation that people seek out for direction, as we continue to piece together our past while recognizing we must also embrace the new ways of the present. I asked my father about the difference between the pole raising in 1969 and the potlatches and feasts that he hosts today, and he explained, "The biggest difference is my generation is the Elders now. I asked, where are my teachers? They're all gone. So, we have to take responsibility now, my generation." Each time that we come together, we continue to add threads to the rope, and as we work together to remember our ancient knowledge, we reinforce our memories and keep our knowledge alive. Though the contemporary potlatch is different than the old ones that were hosted before contact, it continues to serve an integral role in maintaining and strengthening our traditions.

According to Métis father-and-son researchers Jeff and Lee Baker (2010), "Many of us have been severed from our roots and forgotten the deep sense of relation with our ancestors, the planet, and the cosmos, that have characterized human experience for millennia" (98). However, based on what I learned from my father about *sk'ad'a* and ceremony I believe that our connection to our roots has merely been dormant, and as we honour and bring together the pieces of our ancient knowledge and our history, we will revive that connection once again.

I know the *K'awhlaa* dance today because my grandmother put a paper bag over her head so she could teach my father this dance, so this knowledge would remain with us long after her life ended. I will never know why she hid her face with a paper bag when she shared her knowledge of this dance with my father. Sometimes I wonder if it was because of the residual shame that she was made to feel about her ancestral beliefs and practices. Sometimes I wonder if it was to find the courage to pass on the dance. Always I am grateful that she was able to improvise using that paper bag so the dance could be passed on to her grandchildren and their grandchildren and all of the grandchildren in the generations to come, and always I am grateful that my father was there and willing to learn the dance.

A long time ago, my father began to see the gaps in our understanding of our ceremonial practices. He, my uncle, and others were determined to learn more about our ancestral knowledge in order to share it with us. I am grateful that my father believed that every time he hosted a potlatch or feast, it expanded his experience and knowledge. I am grateful that he felt good about giving. As he explained, "I feel good about giving. I feel that I am also learning from it. Every potlatch that I've hosted and co-hosted, I'm learning something from it." Always, I am grateful that my father was able to teach us some of the old ways using potlatch as pedagogy.

Appendix

Feasts and Potlatches Hosted and Co-Hosted by Robert Davidson

1978	Feast to honour apprentices for Charles Edenshaw Memorial longhouse, half-day feast, Old Massett, Haida Gwaii (Co-hosted with Claude Davidson and Reg Davidson)
1980	Tribute to the Living Haida, four-day feast, Old Massett, Haida Gwaii
1981	Children of the Good People, two-day potlatch, New Masset, Haida Gwaii
1989	Every Year the Salmon Come Back, two-day feast, Old Massett, Haida Gwaii
1992	Memorial Potlatch for Arlene Nelson and Arnold Davidson, Old Massett, Haida Gwaii (Co-hosted with Reg Davidson)
1993	Urban Feast: Reconnecting with our Ancestors, two-day feast, Vancouver, BC
1994	Urban Feast: Reconnecting with Our Own Spirit, two-day feast, North Vancouver, BC
1996	Wedding Feast for Robert Davidson and Terri-Lynn Williams-Davidson, Skidegate, BC (Co-hosted with Terri-Lynn Williams-Davidson and each of their clans)
2000	Stone Maul Feast, to honour five people who completed their apprenticeship with Robert Davidson, Sty-wet-tan Hall, Vancouver, BC
2003	Red Potlatch, two-day potlatch, New Masset, Haida Gwaii
2003	Stone Maul Feast, to honour Leslie and Leonard Wells who completed their apprenticeship with Robert Davidson, White Rock, BC

2008   Feast to honour Haida Weavers, New Masset, Haida Gwaii (Co-hosted with Terri-Lynn Williams-Davidson and Reg Davidson)

2008   Feast to honour Haida Weavers, Skidegate, Haida Gwaii (Co-hosted with Terri-Lynn Williams-Davidson and Reg Davidson)

2009   40th Anniversary of 1969 Pole Raising, Old Massett, Haida Gwaii (Co-hosted with Terri-Lynn Williams-Davidson and Reg Davidson)

2016   *Gyaa 'isdlaa* to honour the surviving Haida Clans of Haida Gwaii, two-day potlatch, Old Massett, Haida Gwaii

References

Archibald, Jo-ann. *Indigenous Storywork: Educating the Heart, Mind, Body, and Spirit.* Vancouver, BC: UBC Press, 2008.

Baker, J. J., & Baker, L. M. M. H. "Learning to Relate: Stories from a Father and Son." *Canadian Journal of Native Education, 33,* no. 1 (2010): 98-112.

Battiste, Marie. *Decolonizing Education: Nourishing the Learning Spirit.* Vancouver, BC: Purich Publishing, 2013.

Blackman, Margaret. "Ethnohistoric Changes in the Haida Potlatch Complex. *Arctic Anthropology,* 14, no.1 (1977): 39-53.

———. *During My Time: Florence Edenshaw Davidson, a Haida Woman.* Seattle and London: University of Washington Press, 1982.

Boelscher, Marianne. *The Curtain Within: Haida Social and Mythical Discourse.* Vancouver, BC: UBC Press, 1989.

Boyd, Robert. *The Coming Spirit of Pestilence: Introduced Infectious Diseases and Population Decline among Northwest Coast Indians, 1774–1874.* Vancouver, BC: UBC Press, 1999.

Davidson, Claude. (n.d.). *Haida: A Way of Life,* as told to Sarah Hillis Davidson [unpublished autobiography].

Davidson, Robert. *Four Decades: An Innocent Gesture.* Semiahmoo, BC: Robert Davidson, 2009.

Davidson, Sara Florence. "Responding Aesthetically: Using Artistic Expression and Dialogical Reflection to Transform Adversity." In *The Negotiated Self: Employing Reflexive Inquiry to Explore Teacher Identity,* edited by E. Lyle. Rotterdam, NL: Sense Publishers, 2018.

Davidson, Sara Florence and Robert Davidson. "Make Your Mind Strong: My Father's Insights into Academic Success." *Canadian Journal of Education,* 39, no. 2 (2016: 1–21.

Duff, Wilson. *The Indian History of British Columbia: The Impact of the White Man* (new edition). Victoria, BC: Royal British Columbia Museum, 1997.

Francis, Daniel. *The Imaginary Indian.* Vancouver, Canada: Arsenal Pulp Press, 1992.

Haida Gwaii Singers Society. *Songs of Haida Gwaii: Haida Gwaii Singers Anthology.* Surrey, BC: Haida Gwaii Singers Society, 2008.

Harrison, Charles. *Ancient Warriors of the North Pacific: The Haidas, Their Laws, Customs and Legends, with Some Historical Account of the Queen Charlotte Islands.* London: H. F. & G. Witherby, 1925.

Joseph, Bob. *21 Things You May Not Know about the Indian Act: Helping Canadians Make Reconciliation with Indigenous Peoples a Reality.* Port Coquitlam, BC: Indigenous Relations Press, 2018.

Milloy, John. (2008). "Indian Act Colonialism: A Century of Dishonour, 1869–1969 "Research paper for the Centre for First Nations Governance." Retrieved from: <http://fngovernance.org/ncfng_research/milloy.pdf>

Sealaska Heritage Institute. *A Guide to the Walter Soboleff Building.* Juneau, AK: Sealaska Heritage Institute, 2015.

Steltzer, Ulli and Robert Davidson. *Eagle Transforming: The Art of Robert Davidson.* Vancouver, BC: Douglas & McIntyre, 1994.

Stewart, Hilary. *Robert Davidson: Haida Printmaker.* Vancouver, BC: Douglas & McIntyre, 1979.

Swanton, John R. *Contributions to the Ethnology of the Haida* (Vol. 8, Part I). New York, NY: Memoirs of the American Museum of Natural History, 1905a.

———. *Haida Texts and Myths.* Washington, DC: Government Printing Office, 1905b.

Truth and Reconciliation Commission of Canada. *What We Have Learned: Principles of Truth and Reconciliation,* 2015. Retrieved from: <http://www.trc.ca/websites/trcinstitution/File/2015/Findings/Principles_2015_05_31_web_o.pdf>